# Hegel and Marx

# Hegel and Marx
*Introductory Lectures*

Elie Kedourie

Edited by
Sylvia Kedourie
and
Helen Kedourie

BLACKWELL
Oxford UK & Cambridge USA

Copyright © Sylvia Kedourie 1995

First published 1995

Blackwell Publishers, the publishing imprint of
Basil Blackwell Ltd
108 Cowley Road
Oxford OX4 1JF
UK

Basil Blackwell Inc.
238 Main Street
Cambridge, Massachusetts 02142
USA

All rights reserved. Except for the quotation of short passages for the purposes of criticism and review, no part of this publication may be reproduced, stored in a retrieval system, or transmitted, in any form or by any means, electronic, mechanical, photocopying, recording or otherwise, without the prior permission of the publisher.

Except in the United States of America, this book is sold subject to the condition that it shall not, by way of trade or otherwise, be lent, resold, hired out, or otherwise circulated without the publisher's prior consent in any form of binding or cover other than that in which it is published and without a similar condition including this condition being imposed on the subsequent purchaser.

*British Library Cataloguing in Publication Data*

A CIP catalogue record for this book is available from the British Library.

*Library of Congress Cataloging-in-Publication Data*
Kedourie, Elie.
Hegel and Marx : introductory lectures / Elie Kedourie ; edited by Sylvia Kedourie and Helen Kedourie.
p. cm.
ISBN 0–631–19322–7 (alk. paper). — ISBN 0–631–19323–5 (pbk.)
1. Hegel, Georg Wilhelm Friedrich, 1770–1831. 2. Marx, Karl, 1818–1883. I. Haim, Sylvia G. II. Kedourie, Helen. III. Title.
B2948.K43 1995
193—dc20      94–21501
CIP

Printed in Great Britain by T. J. Press (Padstow) Ltd., Cornwall

This book is printed on acid-free paper

# CONTENTS

|   | | |
|---|---|---|
|   | *Foreword* | vi |
|   | *Acknowledgements* | xi |
| 1 | Introductory Lecture | 1 |
| 2 | Influences on Hegel | 10 |
| 3 | Hegel and Schiller | 23 |
| 4 | Hegel and Lessing | 36 |
| 5 | 'One and All' | 48 |
| 6 | Hegel's Thought | 63 |
| 7 | Hegel and Religion | 77 |
| 8 | Religion | 91 |
| 9 | Property and Personality | 104 |
| 10 | Labour and Civil Society | 115 |
| 11 | Civil Society | 130 |
| 12 | The State | 142 |
| 13 | Feuerbach and Hegel | 152 |
| 14 | Marx and his Criticism of Hegel | 166 |
| 15 | Marx on Hegel | 179 |
|   | *Afterword* | 192 |
|   | *Bibliography* | 202 |
|   | *Index* | 207 |

# FOREWORD

Not long before his sudden death on 29 June 1992, Elie Kedourie told me that his book on Hegel and Marx was finished. My searches so far have not revealed a manuscript newer than the present lectures. These introductory lectures on Hegel and Marx were given at the London School of Economics and Political Science from the mid-1970s.

Elie never wanted to have lectures published in the same form in which he gave them. I have, however, been encouraged by two friends to go ahead and publish what I found. The late Shirley Robin Letwin, who attended the lectures when they were first given, urged me to make them available as they stand, although Elie meant them to form the core of a more polished work. She was noble enough, shortly before she died, to read his handwritten manuscript, and to recommend it for publication.

Another friend, Peter Roberts, with whom I discussed the matter at length, finally persuaded me to publish them. He recalled H. A. L. Fisher's decision to publish posthumously F. W. Maitland's lecture notes, on constitutional history, found among his papers. Fisher acknowledged that Maitland had himself given a categorical no to publishing lectures he had 'written in six months' (F. W. Maitland, *The Constitutional History of England*, ed. H. A. Fisher, Cambridge University Press, 1908, p. v.). Fisher, however, found compelling reasons to publish the lectures. Publication, he argued, could only enhance Maitland's reputation. Maitland's later biographer, H. E. Bell, in *Maitland: A Critical Assessment and Examination* (London, A. & C. Black, 1965) estimated that 'generations of British and American students . . . would have been the poorer for the lack of this volume . . . apart from its absolute value, it had some significance as a background to Maitland's subsequent studies in legal history.'

Elie Kedourie's much shorter present work is likewise a reflection of his broad interests, not only in political philosophy, but also in history and literature. Whereas, of course, Maitland's lectures had been prepared at the beginning of his academic career in 1887, Elie Kedourie's lectures reflect his more mature thinking, having been prepared in mid-career. Elie's study of Hegel and Marx is part of a unity of thought which includes *Nationalism* as well as his writings on Middle Eastern history. As he himself wrote in his preface to a collection of essays on seemingly disparate themes, they are the 'product of one mind', showing 'unity of style, approach and preoccupation' (*The Crossman Confessions*, London, Mansell Publishing Ltd, 1984).

During the last year of his life, as a Fellow at the Woodrow Wilson Center for International Scholars in Washington, he was asked to give one of the lunchtime talks generally attended by most of the other Fellows. Partly as a challenge, because people could not make a connection between his two specialities – the political thought he taught and the history he wrote – he was asked to speak about Hegel in the Middle East. He began by thanking his colleagues for setting him thinking about a connection he had not sought before. I have found the notes of this talk, in which he elucidated the relevance of Hegel's thought to today's world, and I am including them as an afterword.

The lectures, drawing on published material and translation, must be judged for the lucidity and originality with which Elie Kedourie tackled a subject about which whole libraries have been written. The course consisted of 15 hour-and-a-half lectures, and was attended by many colleagues as well as students. It is clear from a glance at the lectures that Elie must have sometimes spoken *ad lib* as they are not all of equal length. The notes which appear at the end of some of the lectures were marginal remarks in the manuscript, and they were obviously reminders to elaborate certain points.

Some indication of the way Elie worked and wrote might be useful in judging a work which he himself would not have considered complete. Having been brought up at a time when paper was a commodity not to be wasted, he would write on any clean paper. Consequently his manuscript could be written on a collection of coloured circulars or even on the back of another manuscript which had already been published. Short of quotes and their page numbers, Elie carried all his material in his head, including, in many cases, the titles of the books from which he was quoting. In the case of the 'lost' Hegel and Marx manuscript, I found among his papers, in the usual unmarked brown envelope, scraps of paper cut out from circulars, each about 2-by-3½ inches, which he had numbered in roman numerals, and on which he had noted lists of page numbers. His method was to put a line across any number the point of which he had already dealt with. Sadly I am unable to use this information to add to his text. The other point which I must highlight about him is that he never sat down to write anything, books included, before he had it ready in his head from beginning to end. It may be that this is what he meant when he told me that the book was finished. His first draft, always hand-written, was always his last draft. There were usually very few corrections – a word changed here and a sentence crossed out there. He very often used to hand his manuscripts to the publishers directly without first having them typed. He very rarely jotted anything down; if he ever did, it was invariably on the back of a used envelope or some other scrap of paper. He was generally engaged in writing a couple of books at the same time, as well as the ubiquitous article.

The lectures are left exactly as he wrote them, and if one looks at chapter 14, it is clear that nothing has been altered even after the collapse of the Soviet Union. The only editing is the addition of chapter headings, and bibliography. The bibliography is drawn from the names of authors mentioned in the margins of the text. We have encountered some difficulty in tracing some of them because Elie often used his own shorthand and we could not always trace all the details. We have therefore left some references incomplete. This is our failure not his.

The books listed represent only a very small proportion of what he read and was still reading until his death. A large number of newly published books on Hegel which he had ordered, arrived too late for him to see. The books listed here relate to immediate points mentioned in the lectures; they do not include books cited in the introductory lecture, nor do they include further editions or translations. In the case of some foreign books which were not available, we relied on Elie's page references without checking them. We have also tried to pinpoint the editions he used whenever possible, but have been unsuccessful in finding the right edition of Marx's *Capital*. We have left these very few references as he gave them.

Finally I would like to express my thanks to a number of friends and colleagues. Kenneth Minogue, John Charvet and Alan Peters were always ready to answer questions. Thanks are also due to T. Fuller, N. Jacobs and I. Dworetzky. William Letwin ferried books back and forth for me and listened with his usual courtesy. Pauline Allen revealed to me the secrets of the LSE library and helped me locate books and check quotations. Diana and Peter Roberts proved the dear and loyal friends they have always been. However, my greatest appreciation goes to Shirley Letwin who, in her frail state, gave me the most generous support and offered great consolation. Our daughter Helen who typed the manuscript, and helped with the work all round, did it all for the love she had for her father and would be embarrassed by formal thanks. I would also like to thank the Wilson Center where Elie found so much contentment during the last year of his life.

Sylvia Kedourie

# ACKNOWLEDGEMENTS

Thanks are due for permission to reproduce the following material which is in copyright:

Christopher BOOKER: Extract from article 'Lost Men of Property', published in the *Daily Telegraph*, © The Telegraph plc, London, 1976. Reprinted by permission of The Telegraph plc.

T. S. ELIOT: Extract from 'Little Gidding' from *Four Quartets*, copyright 1943 by T. S. Eliot and renewed 1971 by Esme Valerie Eliot, and from *Collected Poems 1909–1962* by T. S. Eliot, Faber 1963. Reprinted by permission of Faber & Faber Ltd. and Harcourt Brace & Company.

H. S. HARRIS: Extracts from *Hegel's Development: Towards the Sunlight 1770–1801*, Clarendon Press, 1972. Reprinted by permission of Oxford University Press.

G. W. F. HEGEL: Extracts from *The Philosophy of Right*, translated with notes by T. M. Knox, OUP 1945. Reprinted by permission of Oxford University Press. Extracts from *Political Writings*, translated by T. M. Knox, edited by Z. A. Pelczynski, OUP 1964. Reprinted by permission of Oxford University Press. Extracts from *The Phenomenology of Mind*, translated by J. B. Baillie, Allen & Unwin 1971. Reprinted by permission of Routledge. Extracts from *Early Theological Writings*, translated and edited by T. M. Knox and Richard Kroner, University of Chicago Press 1948 (reissued in 1961 by Harper Torch Books).

Friedrich HÖLDERLIN: Extracts from 'New World', 'The Archipelago' and 'Bread and Wine' from *Hölderlin: His Poems*, translated by Michael Hamburger, Harvill Press, an imprint of HarperCollins Publishers Ltd, © Harvill Press 1952. Reprinted by permission of HarperCollins Publishers. Extracts from *Hyperion*, translated by Willard R. Trask, translation Copyright © 1965 by Willard R. Trask, foreword by Alexander Gode-von Aesch, copyright © 1965 by The New English Library Ltd. Used by permission of Dutton Signet, a division of Penguin Books USA, Inc.

Karl MARX: Extracts from *Early Writings*, translated by Rodney Livingstone and Gregor Benton, Penguin Books 1975, translation copyright © Rodney Livingstone and Gregor Benton, 1974, Selection copyright © New Left Review, 1974. Reproduced by permission of Penguin Books Ltd.

Karl MARX and Josef ENGELS: Extracts from *The German Ideology* Part 1, edited by C. J. Arthur, Lawrence & Wishart Ltd, London 1970. Reprinted by permission of Lawrence & Wishart Ltd.

J. C. Friedrich von SCHILLER: Extracts from *On the Aesthetic Education of Man: In a Series of Letters*, edited and translated with Introduction, Commentary and Glossary by Elizabeth M. Wilkinson and L. A. Willoughby, Clarendon Press 1967. Reprinted by permission of Oxford University Press.

## Acknowledgements

Paul VALÉRY: Extract from 'The Graveyard by the Sea' from *The Collected Works*, translated by David Paul, © 1960 renewed 1988 by Princeton University Press, British Edition Routledge & Kegan Paul 1971. Reprinted by permission of Routledge and Princeton University Press.

Despite every effort to trace and contact copyright holders before publication, this has not always been possible. If notified, the publisher will be pleased to rectify any errors or omissions at the earliest opportunity.

# 1
# INTRODUCTORY LECTURE

The political thought of Hegel and Marx is a non-committal title particularly suitable for this particular exploration. We might say that these lectures will be an attempt to expose to view the layers of significance which may be found in this copula *and* where it joins these two particular names. We can start with the most prevalent view as to the meaning of the expression 'Hegel and Marx'.

It is widely believed that Marx is an enormously important thinker who has provided a key to the understanding of the course of history, and particularly to the understanding of modern economics and politics. It is also believed that Marx's achievement has something to do with Hegel's philosophical legacy – that Marx, to use a term which in this context is particularly apt, *appropriated* Hegel's ideas, subjected them to examination and criticism, discarded what was useless or erroneous, and used the sound parts which remained after this scrutiny as a means for shedding light on the hidden, mysterious and – to use another term which is appropriate in this context – the *mystifying* processes of social life. In other words, that Hegel had been standing on his head, and Marx came and stood him the right way up.

But this account, assuming that it is true, is a very cursory one, and thus not very satisfactory. To say that Marx stood Hegel the right way up is to make a (metaphorical) statement about intellectual history, about intellectual influences and intellectual filiations. But in intellectual history (as in any other kind of history) detail is of the essence, and for us to make sense of some such statement as that Marx stood Hegel on his head we have to show *in detail* how this came about, which particular and specific ideas of Hegel's were transmitted to Marx, and in what manner (to borrow an appropriate term from the Hegelian vocabulary) they were mediated from the one to the other thinker.

When we attempt to do this, we immediately find that we have to deal with, and surmount, certain difficulties. My business is with the *political thought* of Hegel and Marx. Political thought is a wide expression and can embrace a wide range of writings, from comment on current political affairs to a systematic consideration of the character and modalities of the political association. Now so far as concerns Hegel, his writings do cover such a wide range. For instance at the beginning of his career as a writer, in 1798, he wrote an essay (which he did not himself publish) entitled 'On the Recent Domestic Affairs of Württemberg', while one of the very last things he wrote before he died in 1831 was another article on 'The English Reform Bill'. Hegel was always very interested in current affairs and indeed for a short time acted as a newspaper editor. It was he who said that the newspaper was modern man's version of morning prayers. But of course he was not a mere breathless BBC commentator skating precariously on the surface of events and keeping his balance by clutching at one headline after another. This can easily be discovered by looking at the volume of his *Political Writings* translated by T. M. Knox and edited by Z. A.

Pelczynski. But though one can see that underlying these pieces there is a complex, sophisticated and systematic view of politics, yet one could not possibly work out from these pieces Hegel's teaching on politics as he set it out in one of the four major philosophical treatises which he himself published in his lifetime, namely *The Philosophy of Right*, the first edition of which came out in 1821.

Marx too published a large number of occasional pieces on politics, which again are not mere current affairs, and again it is possible to extrapolate from such pieces a systematic account of Marx's view of the political association, but as we all know such extrapolations are somewhat risky and unsatisfactory. And the fact remains that Marx did not write an equivalent to Hegel's *Philosophy of Right*. The task, however, is made easier by the fact that at the outset of his career Marx did comment specifically on a number of paragraphs of the *Philosophy of Right* in a writing of 1843 which he himself did not publish, and which was published subsequently (in 1927) under the title 'Critique of Hegel's Doctrine of the State'. To help us understand Marx's view of politics, and particularly his view of Hegel's ideas on politics, we have another very important writing of his of 1844 known as 'Economic and Philosophical Manuscripts', which was first published in 1932. And to it we may add a number of pieces which Marx himself did publish, and in particular the article entitled 'A Contribution to the Critique of Hegel's Philosophy of Right. Introduction', which came out in the *Franco-German Yearbooks* in 1844.

But it remains a fact that in considering the *political thought* of Hegel *and* Marx we are considering two unequal or let us say asymmetrical bodies of thought. And we may come to think that this fact makes for difficulty in our attempt to understand exactly and fully the connections and mediations between the political thought of these two writers, but also, and perhaps more important, we may come to the conclusion that the fact that Hegel did write a systematic treatise on the political association, and that Marx did not, tells us something very significant about the substantive character of their respective views of the state and of the character of political activity. To adopt a Marxist locution, we may come to think that it is perhaps *not by accident* that Hegel considered the state and politics at length, and that Marx did not do so.

Thus a simple inspection of the political writings of Hegel and Marx – at their various levels of abstraction –indicates that the enterprise of studying the *political thought* of Hegel *and* Marx is bound to be difficult and problematic. Other features add to this difficulty, such as the philosophical vocabulary and style of these two thinkers. Hegel trained in history, the classics and theology, and his earliest writings, which he himself left unpublished, dealt (on the face of it) with theological and religious issues, so much so that Nohl, the editor who first published these writings, entitled the book in which he collected them *Hegels theologische Jugendschriften*, and this view of them was taken by T. M. Knox and Richard Kroner when they entitled the extensive selections which they translated from Nohl's collection and published in 1948 as *Early Theological Writings*. It was at the age of 31, in 1801, when he had already thought deeply and with much originality about both religion and politics, that he published his first philosophical essay – which was also the first writing that he published. This essay is entitled *The Difference between the Philosophical Systems of Fichte and Schelling*. A letter of about this time to his friend and contemporary at the Tübingen theological seminary, F. W. J. Schelling (1775–1854), gives us an idea of the reasons which led Hegel to take up philosophy:

> In my scientific development, which began from the more subordinate needs of men, I was bound to be driven on to science, and the ideal of my youth had to be transformed at the same time into reflective form, into a system.

This passage is followed by another which constitutes for us an ironical commentary on the usual allegation that Hegel's mystical and mystificatory philosophy was brought down to earth by Marx. This allegation of course has its origin in the last and best-known of Marx's famous 11 theses on Feuerbach, which is to the effect that 'philosophers have only *interpreted* the world, in various ways; the point is to *change* it' (1845). The passage from Hegel's letter to Schelling which follows the words I have already quoted, expressed, 45 years before Marx, the very same aspiration: 'I ask myself now,' Hegel wrote, 'while I am still occupied with this, *how I am to find a way back to intervention in the life of men.*'

In his letter to Schelling, Hegel speaks of the need he felt to transform 'the ideal of my youth' into a system. We may perhaps translate this as the need to place his thoughts on society, religion and politics into the widest context. This widest of all contexts was precisely philosophy, which would serve to make absolutely transparent, coherent and necessary the world and our experience of it. This accounting for, this making absolutely transparent all experience and knowledge was indeed the aspiration of the philosophy of Hegel's day, as practised by Hegel's friend Schelling and by Fichte (1762–1814) (whom Schelling at that point very much admired). Fichte in turn had drawn his inspiration from Kant (1724–1804), the incoherences of whose philosophy he attempted to remedy.

When Hegel therefore came to philosophy he found ready to hand a way of doing philosophy, a vocabulary of philosophy, and a consensus about what constituted a philosophical problem and what possible shape solutions to such a problem could take. Hegel took all this over, and though his philosophical vocabulary and many of his most important philosophical notions have their source outside philosophy, in theology or history, yet there is no doubt that Hegel's own philosophizing is deeply marked by the Kantian, Fichtian or Schellingian manner and vocabulary. This manner and vocabulary are in themselves difficult enough, one may perhaps say needlessly difficult and complicated, but what increases the difficulty for us in the English-speaking world is that the vocabulary and the manner of philosophizing which characterize Fichte's and Hegel's writings have become unfamiliar under the long dominance of G. E. Moore, Bertrand Russell, logical positivism and analytical philosophy. Let us remember that the interest in Hegel which is today to be seen on all sides is something very recent indeed, a matter of the last few decades. So that to understand Hegel's ideas in his philosophical works, say in the *Phenomenology* or the *Philosophy of Right*, ideas in themselves anyway subtle and very difficult to lay hold of, has to us, because of our circumstances, become an even more difficult and taxing exercise.

Another difficulty which stands in the way of a proper study of Hegel's political thought relates to Hegel and his reputation. When Hegel died in 1831 he was professor of philosophy at Berlin, and his philosophy was by and large the dominant one in German universities. After his death many people came to accuse him of having been the apologist and mouthpiece of Prussian reaction and obscurantism. This was most notably argued in a book on *Hegel and his Times*, published in 1857 by Rudolf Haym. Such accusations had no real basis so far as Hegel's own political sympathies and political activities were concerned. Hegel's own writings, whether occasional or otherwise, are enough to show this. And what the writings show may be confirmed by Hegel's own activities. Two recent books by Jacques d'Hondt may be mentioned here: *Hegel secret* and *Hegel en son temps*. But Hegel's reputation as a sinister reactionary persisted and grew. Indeed for large numbers of readers in the English-speaking world Hegel appears as the harbinger of militarism and Nazism. It is not part of this course of lectures to discuss in any detail these attacks on Hegel, but I ought to draw your attention to an article by Professor Walter Kaufmann which is a critique of Popper's way with Hegel: 'The Hegel Myth and its Method' in *The Owl and the Nightingale*, reprinted in Walter Kaufmann, ed., *Hegel's Political Philosophy* (New York, 1970).

A third difficulty which we may encounter in studying the political thought of Hegel and Marx has to do with Marx. In some sense or another what Marx thought and wrote has a connection with what is called Marxism. Marxism is not the equivalent of what might be called Hegelianism. If by Hegelianism we mean a body of philosophical thought derived from and built on what Hegel wrote, then Marxism is much more than its counterpart. Marxism was adopted as the *ideology* of many political movements, and in the twentieth century became the official orthodoxy in the Soviet Union, in those countries under its control and influence, and of China. Marxism thus became involved with party struggles, the pursuit of power, rivalries between states, and among political leaders. Great interests were sometimes at stake in this or that interpretation of what Marx said or meant. In his *Oriental Despotism* Wittfogel discusses the Asiatic mode of production and whether such a category was useful in understanding the Russian past. And since the interest in Hegel's thought is, among a great many people, a consequence of passionate interest in Marx, and since the interest in Marx stemmed from an interest in Marxism as an ideology and an adjunct of political power, then here were powerful barriers to the understanding of both Marx and Hegel.

An examination of the political thought of Hegel and Marx involves, then, for a start, an examination of Hegel's political thought. But what is Hegel's political thought? In this context it is obviously the thought as transmitted through various mediations to Marx: the political thought as it appears principally in *The Philosophy of Right*. But we ourselves are much better placed to understand the character of Hegel's political thought than Marx was. And this is because Marx did not have the benefit of access to Hegel's unpublished writings. These writings were first systematically examined by Wilhelm Dilthey in his work *Die Jugendgeschichte Hegels*, published in 1905, the writings themselves being published by Dilthey's disciple Hermann Nohl in 1907. If we examine these writings, then we detect in them a powerful impulse to change rather than to interpret the world, an impulse such that we might come to think that the 30-year-old philosopher-in-the-making, Hegel, who asked – in his letter to Schelling - 'How am I to find a way back to intervention in the life of men' had already thought seriously and to some purpose about 'intervention in the life of men'. If this is the case, then we have uncovered another, larger meaning in the expression 'the political thought of Hegel and Marx'. If we look at that political thought of Hegel's which Marx did not know, then we will find ourselves examining the similarities – which we will find to be very significant – between Marx's political thought and that of the young Hegel. My concern here is not to discern ways of transmission and mediation, but to compare and to contrast, to ask in what ways the political thought of the young Hegel was similar to Marx's and how the political thought of the older Hegel went beyond that of his youth, and thus also perhaps beyond that of Marx.

Our business, then, for more than one reason, is, to start with, with the young Hegel's universe of discourse, with the intellectual, social and political context in which he found himself and to which he reacted – with high intelligence and great passion. This may seem a very roundabout way to proceed but in its justification one may quote two statements by Hegel himself. In a letter to Victor Cousin, who asked him for a concise statement of his philosophy, Hegel wrote: 'Sir . . . these things are not to be expressed succinctly.' Again, in *The Philosophy of Right* – and elsewhere – Hegel stated that philosophy is a circle. Among the possible corollaries of this statement is that the straight line will be sure to lead you nowhere.

# 2
# INFLUENCES ON HEGEL

Hegel was born in Stuttgart in 1770. His father was a financial official in the Duchy of Württemberg. From 1780 to 1788 he attended the Stuttgart Gymnasium, and from 1788 to 1793 he was a scholar at the Tübinger Stift, part of the University of Tübingen. There he met two other scholars who became and continued to be close friends and whose influence on Hegel's intellectual development was very great. The first has already been mentioned: F. W. J. Schelling, who was five years his junior but who was immensely clever as a schoolboy and undergraduate. The other was J. C. F. Hölderlin, who was born in the same year as Hegel and who was to die in 1843, thus surviving Hegel by 12 years.

Students at the Tübinger Stift followed a course which qualified them for positions in the Church, in teaching or in government. In his home, as in the gymnasium and in the Stift, Hegel was in contact with the public affairs of the day. His education gave him an entrance into the classical world, the influence of which, particularly that of Greek literature and philosophy, was both deep and lasting. His education also acquainted him necessarily with current issues in Protestant theology, a theology which had been trying for some time to come to terms with the Enlightenment and to answer its intellectual challenge, and when possible to use the new conceptions and the new philosophy in order to defend Christianity and save its traditional dogmas as much as possible from the ravages of scepticism and unbelief. Between 1793 and 1797 Hegel was a tutor in the household of an aristocratic family in Berne in Switzerland. His writings and his letters (in particular to his friends Schelling and Hölderlin) have survived, and they provide us with a detailed and vivid picture of his intellectual preoccupations and of the coming-to-be of certain key ideas and concepts which he was to develop and deepen in his later, published, writings. In 1797 his friend Hölderlin obtained for him a similar post in a well-to-do household in Frankfurt, where Hölderlin himself had a similar post with another such family. He was to remain in Frankfurt for three years. For Hegel the period in Frankfurt was happier and more stimulating than the time at Berne; Hegel all through his life seemed to have been a sociable and friendly man who liked to go to parties, to dance and join in a game of cards. In Frankfurt he had a circle in which he felt at home, and, more important, he had the advantage of intellectual stimulation and intellectual exchanges on political and philosophical issues. Frankfurt was also a commercial metropolis far more open to the world and its intellectual currents than ever Berne could be. It was in Frankfurt that Hegel began to show his originality as a thinker, and to grapple with contemporary political issues. It was during this period that he wrote the essay 'On the Recent Domestic Affairs of Württemberg' mentioned in the last lecture. It was there that he published (anonymously in 1798) a translation from the French with an introduction and notes of a work by Jean-Jacques Cart, a French Girondin lawyer, the title of which will give an idea of its contents and of Hegel's political attitudes and sympathies: *Confidential Letters concerning the former Constitutional Relation of the Wadtland (Pays de Vaud) to the State of Berne. A Complete Exposition of the earlier Oligarchy of the Berne Nobility.*

In Frankfurt we also have evidence that Hegel devoted a great deal of time to the study of economics; reading Adam Smith, who may have studied at Iena, and, as has been recently shown, more important for the decisive influence it had on his subsequent thought, a work by the Scotsman Sir James Steuart, *An Enquiry into the Principles of Political Oeconomy: Being an Essay on the Science of Domestic Policy in Free Nations* published in 1767 and translated into German in 1769–72.

During this extraordinarily fruitful period Hegel also continued his studies in religious history and theology, and in these studies we can already see the influence of his thinking on economic activity and the social change associated with it. We also see a decisive departure in his views about Christianity and about religion and society in general. It was towards the end of his Frankfurt period that Hegel wrote his letter to Schelling which I have already quoted and in which he said that he had begun to feel that the 'ideal of my youth had to be transformed at the same time into reflective form, into a system'. It was as a result of his political, economic and religious studies that the 30-year-old Hegel felt the need for working out a philosophical system which would enable him to have a clear view of the map of human knowledge, and of the relation between practice and theory.

Schelling was then teaching at the University of Iena, and it was with his help that Hegel moved to Iena where he began his career as a philosopher. He established himself as a *Privatdozent* in the University, that is, an unsalaried lecturer who was directly paid by the students who came to his lectures. He remained a *Privatdozent* from 1801 to 1805 when he was appointed to a salaried teaching post as a *professor extraordinarius*. It was during this Iena period that he published his first philosophical work, *The Difference between the Philosophical Systems of Fichte and Schelling* and some fairly long articles in a philosophical journal on which he collaborated with Schelling, among which *On the Scientific Manner of Studying Natural Law* and *Faith and Knowledge*. But much more interesting for us in this context are the lectures which he gave, the notes for which were published only in this century. They are known by the titles given by their editors: *System der Sittlichkeit 1803, Realphilosophie I 1803–4* and *Realphilosophie II 1805–6*. It was towards the end of the Iena period in 1805–6 that Hegel wrote *The Phenomenology of Spirit* which was published in 1807 and which indicated to the world at large that an original and powerful philosophical voice was speaking.

The Iena period in Hegel's life came to an end in 1806 with the battle of Iena at which Napoleon defeated the Prussian Army. Hegel wrote the last words of *The Phenomenology of Spirit* on the eve of the battle. The ensuing disorders forced him to flee from the city, carrying with him to safety the second half of the manuscript of *The Phenomenology of Spirit*.

In a letter to a friend after the battle of Iena, Hegel referred to the entry of the French troops into the city with Napoleon at their head and wrote that he saw the soul of the world riding on horseback. Whatever Hegel meant exactly by this expression, it at any rate shows how much he was impressed with the notion that he was living through a decisive juncture in human history. But such a feeling could not have been something new for Hegel or indeed for his circle. The French Revolution had broken out at the end of his first session at the

Tübinger Stift and the political convulsions which took place in France, Germany and Europe between 1789 and the battle of Iena have to be borne in mind if we are to understand the character of Hegel's political thought. This is so simply because he himself was passionately and continuously interested in politics. He and his friends Hölderlin and Schelling were highly sympathetic to the ideals and aims of the Revolution at its beginning. And it was not only at the battle of Iena that the feeling was abroad – in Hegel's case as in others' – that great and fundamental changes were taking place or about to take place in a European society, which to many of the most influential thinkers, whether French or German, seemed to have outlived itself, to have become ossified, petrified, a constraint on living human energies, a society which was corrupt, cynical and heartless. Rousseau's *Discourse on Inequality*, Beaumarchais's Figaro, and Rameau's nephew in Diderot's tale, all express before the revolution the feeling that this was a society for which there was little to be said, and whose rottenness could not go on. Again, since we are considering a German thinker (though Hegel was very well read in, and much appreciated, the French literature of his day; he quotes from Diderot's *Le Neveu de Rameau* in *The Phenomenology of Spirit*), we may mention two expressions among the intellectual classes of the German-speaking world of the widespread feeling that things were on the move, that great changes were impending. Goethe gave his verdict on the battle of Valmy of September 1792, a decisive event in which the French Revolutionary armies defeated the Allied armies ranged against them. He was present, and after the battle he was summoned by his master, the Duke of Weimar, and asked what he thought of it all: 'From this time and place dates the beginning of a new epoch in the history of the world.' The other expression is found in Lessing's *The Education of the*

*Human Race*, 1780, in which we have a progressive vision of history, a history of humanity on the ascent, increasing in enlightenment and in happiness and destined to outgrow the intellectual habits and the religious dogmas which so far Providence had found necessary that men should believe.

But it is possible for us to be more exact and specific about the particular features of German society which impressed Hegel, his friends and his contemporaries among the educated classes as particularly unsatisfactory. If we were to choose a few words to describe the situation as they saw it, then these words would include rift, division, split, fragmentation, scission. These words can be seen to apply to the most important aspects of life in the German-speaking world. There was a rift between the educated classes, who were full of the Enlightenment ideals of the French literature in which these ideals had been first expressed (of these Frederick the Great with his admiration for French culture and his contempt for German language and literature may stand as exemplar), and, on the other hand, those who were not educated, who did not understand French or appreciate French literature. In other words there was no common national culture in Germany as by that time there was in France, Spain or England. J. G. Herder (1744–1803), who felt very strongly what he considered to be the tyranny of French ideas and literary forms, put it this way: in contrast with Germany, the Greek language, in classical times, 'was spoken by all the children, understood by everyone, and sung in the street by both poets and fools. The gods were the gods of the people, even of the rabble. History and heroic deeds were things cherished and possessed by all the people.'

This rift in the world of culture was accompanied by division in the world of politics. The German-speaking world was supposed to be unified by what we might call the federal institutions of the Holy Roman Empire. But these institutions had fallen into decay a long time ago, and the political reality was of a multitude of states, some very large and powerful like Prussia and some minuscule statelets hardly larger than a nobleman's country estate. Ninety-four spiritual and lay princes, 103 counts, 40 prelates and 51 free towns exercised between them sovereignty over German-speaking lands. By the end of the eighteenth century the political ideal of many of these rulers – in response to widespread currents in European political thinking – was what has been called enlightened absolutism. There was believed to be a science of government, a *Kameralwissenschaft*, which, if mastered by the rulers, enabled them to provide and apportion scientifically welfare and happiness to all their subjects. Politics was seen as a science and government a machine run on scientific lines. This no doubt was a mere bookish aspiration or affectation but the attempt to put it into practice was bound to conflict with such constitutional and representative devices as still subsisted in the German-speaking world, and to increase the gulf between enlightened rulers and the recipients of their scientific ministrations.

Yet another division was to be observed in the religious field, a division which was the legacy of the Thirty Years' War and of the settlement which followed it as embodied in the Treaty of Westphalia of 1648. The principle of this settlement which was the outcome of a long war of attrition which ravaged and ruined Germany was *cuius regio eius religio*, that is, that the religion of the ruler should be the religion of the state. This was to enshrine religious compulsion and religious uniformity into the public law of Germany, and therefore to introduce into religion a powerful leaven of corruption and decay. This was done for the sake of peace, and the peace that resulted was, religiously speaking, the peace of the cemetery. Religion as an affair of state could not also be an affair of the heart. To the deadening effect of this religious settlement was to be joined the corrosive scepticism about Christian creeds induced by enlightened criticism.

This fragmentation of life in its various aspects found its culmination and highest point of concentration in Kant's philosophy, the apex of all the thought of the Enlightenment, which, from a certain vantage-point, could well be called the philosophy of rift and fragmentation. For in Kant's world there was a great gulf fixed in principle between the appearance of things (which was all we could know of them) and their reality (whatever that was), between knowledge and morality, between God, of whom we could know nothing except that his existence was a necessary postulate, and God's creation, between nature and virtue, between inclination and duty. To any intelligent and sensitive man this state of affairs in the world of politics, culture, religion and philosophy was bound to appear intolerable. If there was anything in the contention that history was not immobile, that men by taking thought could diagnose the evil and provide a cure for it – and both these contentions seemed to thinking men at the end of the eighteenth century to be eminently reasonable and indeed obvious – then it ought to be possible to heal the rift in the soul and in society alike, and to create or re-create spiritual unity and social union in which reason and inclination, science and belief, rulers and the ruled would not be estranged from, would not wage war against, one another. And we may say that this became the central issue of German thought, and subsequently of European thought at the end of the eighteenth and during the nineteenth century.

My central preoccupation in these lectures is with Hegel and Marx. Hegel lived from 1770 to 1831, and

Marx from 1818 to 1883. Looked at in terms of generations we can see a pattern in the transmission of these issues. These problems were mediated to Hegel and his circle through the work of Kant (1724–1804), G. E. Lessing (1729–81), J. C. F. von Schiller (1759–1805) and J. G. Fichte (1762–1814), and from Hegel to Marx through the writings of some Hegelian disciples (who in their writings reacted, sometimes violently, against the Master), of whom the most important was Ludwig Feuerbach (1804–72).

I have mentioned the name of Schiller as one of those whose thought mediated to Hegel the central issues of philosophy and politics. The means by which this mediation took place was Schiller's treatise *On the Aesthetic Education of Man: In a Series of Letters*, which first appeared in his newly founded journal *Die Horen* (The Graces) in 1795, when Hegel was in Berne. In a letter to Schelling in April 1795, Hegel said of the first 16 (of the 27) letters which had by then appeared that they were a 'masterpiece', and the letters also made as profound an impression on Hölderlin, to whom Schiller was hero. And it was directly from Schiller as well as through Hölderlin that certain key ideas about the conditions necessary to a harmonious undivided life came to the young Hegel, to be considered and assimilated by him into his own thought. The best way of understanding these key ideas is to consider Schiller's own argument.[1]

Fifth Letter

(5) The cultivated classes, on the other hand, offer the even more repugnant spectacle of lethargy, and of a depravation of character which offends the more because culture itself is its source. I no longer recall which of the ancient or modern philosophers it was who remarked that the nobler a thing is, the more repulsive it

is when it decays; but we shall find that this is no less true in the moral sphere. The child of Nature, when he breaks loose, turns into a madman; the creature of Civilisation into a knave. That Enlightenment of the mind, which is the not altogether groundless boast of our refined classes, has had on the whole so little of an ennobling influence on feeling and character that it has tended rather to bolster up depravity by providing it with the support of precepts. We disown Nature in her rightful sphere only to submit to her tyranny in the moral, and while resisting the impact she makes upon our senses are content to take over her principles. The sham propriety of our manners refuses her the first say – which would be pardonable – only to concede to her in our materialistic ethics the final and decisive one. In the very bosom of the most exquisitely developed social life egotism has founded its system, and without ever acquiring therefrom a heart that is truly sociable, we suffer all the contagions and afflictions of society. We subject our free judgement to its despotic opinion, our feeling to its fantastic customs, our will to its seductions; only our caprice do we uphold against its sacred rights. Proud self-sufficiency contracts the heart of the man of the world, a heart which in natural man still often beats in sympathy; and as from a city in flames each man seeks only to save from the general destruction his own wretched belongings. Only by completely abjuring sensibility can we, so it is thought, be safe from its aberrations; and the ridicule which often acts as a salutary chastener of the enthusiast is equally unsparing in its desecration of the noblest feeling. Civilisation, far from setting us free, in fact creates some new need with every new power it develops in us. The fetters of the physical tighten even more alarmingly, so that fear of losing what we have stifles even the most burning impulse towards improvement, and the maxim of passive obedience passes for the supreme wisdom of life. Thus do we see the spirit of the age wavering between perversity and brutality, between unnaturalness and mere nature, between superstition and moral unbelief; and it is only through an equilibrium of evils that it is still sometimes kept within bounds.

Sixth Letter

(3) . . . With us, one might almost be tempted to assert, the various faculties appear as separate in practice as they are distinguished by the psychologist in theory, and we see not merely individuals, but whole classes of men, developing but one part of their potentialities, while of the rest, as in stunted growths, only vestigial traces remain.

(4) I do not underrate the advantages which the human race today, considered as a whole and weighed in the balance of intellect, can boast in the face of what is best in the ancient world. But it has to take up the challenge in serried ranks, and let whole measure itself against whole. What individual Modern could sally forth and engage, man against man, with an individual Athenian for the prize of humanity?

(5) Whence this disadvantage among individuals when the species as a whole is at such an advantage? Why was the individual Greek qualified to be the representative of his age, and why can no single Modern venture as much? Because it was from all-unifying Nature that the former, and from the all-dividing Intellect that the latter, received their respective forms.

(6) It was civilisation itself which inflicted this wound upon modern man. Once the increase of empirical knowledge, and more exact modes of thought, made sharper divisions between the sciences inevitable, and once the increasingly complex machinery of State necessitated a more rigorous separation of ranks and occupations, then the inner unity of human nature was severed too, and a disastrous conflict set its harmonious powers at variance. The intuitive and the speculative

understanding now withdrew in hostility to take up positions in their respective fields, whose frontiers they now began to guard with jealous mistrust; and with this confining of our activity to a particular sphere we have given ourselves a master within, who not infrequently ends by suppressing the rest of our potentialities. While in the one a riotous imagination ravages the hard-won fruits of the intellect, in another the spirit of abstraction stifles the fire at which the heart should have warmed itself and the imagination been kindled.

(7) This disorganization which was first started within man by civilisation and learning, was made complete and universal by the new spirit of government. . . . That polypoid character of the Greek States, in which every individual enjoyed an independent existence but could, when need arose, grow into the whole organism, now made way for an ingenious clockwork, in which, out of the piecing together of innumerable but lifeless parts, a mechanical kind of collective life ensued. . . . But even that meagre, fragmentary participation, by which individual members of the State are still linked to the Whole, does not depend upon forms which they spontaneously prescribe for themselves (for how could one entrust to their freedom of action a mechanism so intricate and so fearful of light and enlightenment?); it is dictated to them with meticulous exactitude by means of a formulary which inhibits all freedom of thought. The dead letter takes the place of living understanding, and a good memory is a safer guide than imagination and feeling.

(8) When the community makes his office the measure of the man; when in one of its citizens it prizes nothing but memory, in another a mere tabularizing intelligence, in a third only mechanical skill; when, in the one case, indifferent to character, it insists exclusively on knowledge, yet is, in another, ready to condone any amount of obscurantist thinking as long as it is accompanied by a

spirit of order and law-abiding behaviour; when, moreover, it insists on special skills being developed with a degree of intensity which is only commensurate with its readiness to absolve the individual citizen from developing himself in extensity – can we wonder that the remaining aptitudes of the psyche are neglected in order to give undivided attention to the one which will bring honour and profit? . . .

(9) Thus little by little the concrete life of the Individual is destroyed in order that the abstract idea of the Whole may drag out its sorry existence, and the State remains for ever a stranger to its citizens since at no point does it ever make contact with their feeling. Forced to resort to classification in order to cope with the variety of its citizens, and never to get an impression of humanity except through representation at second hand, the governing section ends up by losing sight of them altogether, confusing their concrete reality with a mere construct of the intellect; while the governed cannot but receive with indifference laws which are scarcely, if at all, directed to them as persons. Weary at last of sustaining bonds which the State does so little to facilitate, positive society begins (this has long been the fate of most European States) to disintegrate into a state of primitive morality, in which public authority has become but one party more, to be hated and circumvented by those who make authority necessary, and only obeyed by such as are capable of doing without it.

## Notes

1 The following extracts appeared in the manuscript without comment. The translation used by E. Kedourie is F. Schiller, *On the Aesthetic Education of Man: In a Series of Letters* ed. and trans. with introduction, commentary and glossary by Elizabeth M. Wilkinson and L. A. Willoughby (Oxford, Clarendon Press, 1967).

# 3

# HEGEL AND SCHILLER

Two passages from the fifth and sixth letters of Schiller's *Letters on the Aesthetic Education of Man* were given in the last lecture. Here I shall concentrate on a few sentences.

In the fifth letter, paragraph 27, Schiller writes 'Civilisation, far from setting us free by its very progress creates new needs and enslaves us to them.' The result is that 'In the very bosom of the most exquisitely developed social life egotism has founded its system' and 'we suffer all the contagions and afflictions of society.'

Schiller argues that by its very operation civilization introduces a rift between men in society, and a rift within man himself. There is no wholeness in individuals any more. Each man has to specialize in some one thing and let the rest of his faculties atrophy. He cannot live his life as a whole. And these incomplete men have no living, but only a mechanical relation to one another. And this mechanical relation is seen in all its unfreedom, constriction, and unhappy sterility in 'the new spirit of government' described as 'an ingenious clockwork, in which, out of the piecing together of innumerable but lifeless parts, a mechanical kind of collective life ensued'. In this inhuman state 'enjoyment [is] divorced from labour, the means from the end, the effort from the reward.'[1]

We should be right to see in this passage a prefiguration and, more, an inspiration of what Hegel was to say very shortly afterwards, and what Marx was in his turn to say many years later.

But to the rift which civilization has produced in man and in the state, we have to add yet another rift which we can say predates civilization, which one can say is original to man himself: 'Nature deals no better with man than with the rest of her works: she acts for him as long as he is yet incapable of acting for himself as a free intelligence.' When nature acts for man then he is under 'a blind compulsion'. But man is a free intelligence and therefore with this 'state of compulsion, born of what nature destined him to be . . . he neither could nor can rest content as a Moral Being'. Thus, for example, 'he withdraws from the dominion of blind necessity,' he 'obliterates by means of morality, and ennobles by means of beauty, the crude character imposed by physical need upon sexual love'.[2]

Because man is subject to nature, but also a free intelligence, he cannot remain imprisoned by the shackles which nature imposes. Even while he is immersed in the mere life of sense, he feels dissatisfaction, and begins to obey the promptings of morality and the moral law. But because he is still immersed in the life of sense, the glimmerings of what the moral life is produces in man yet another rift. For the mere life of the senses, nature and the world are unproblematical. Between man and nature there is, at this primitive stage, a unity which no self-questioning disturbs. But when the moral law

> first makes its appearance in the life of sense [it] cannot escape such perversion. Since its voice is merely inhibitory, and against the interest of his animal self-love, it is bound to seem like something external to

himself as long as he has not reached the point of regarding his self-love as the thing that is really external to him, and the voice of his reason as his true self. Hence he merely feels the fetters which reason lays upon him, not the infinite liberation which it is capable of affording him. Without suspecting the dignity of the lawgiver within, he merely experiences its coercive force and feels the impotent resistance of a powerless subject. Because in his experience the sense-drive precedes the moral, he assigns to the law of necessity a beginning in time too, a *positive* origin, and through this most unfortunate of all errors makes the unchangeable and eternal in himself into an accidental product of the transient. He persuades himself into regarding the concepts of right and wrong as *statutes* introduced by some will, not as something valid in themselves for all eternity. Just as in the explanation of particular natural phenomena he goes beyond Nature and seeks outside of it what can only be found in the laws inherent within it, so too, in the explanation of the moral world, he goes beyond reason and forfeits his humanity by seeking a Godhead along these same lines.[3]

At the time when this passage appeared in print the young Hegel in Berne was engaged in writing a radical critique of traditional Christian dogma, to which the editor of his early writings, Nohl, has given the title *The Positivity of the Christian Religion*. The burden of his critique is that Jesus' followers denatured his teaching by making it *positive*. Towards the beginning of the writing he asks:

> How could we have expected a teacher like Jesus to afford any inducement to the creation of a positive religion, i.e. a religion which is grounded in authority and puts man's worth not at all, or at least not wholly in morals? . . . [Jesus] urged not a virtue grounded on authority (which is either meaningless or a direct contradiction in terms), but a free virtue springing from man's own being.[4]

We shall come back to this writing of Hegel's, but now all that we need note is this idea common to Schiller and to Hegel of a *positive* religion, that is, a religion which man believes to be ordained by a higher being outside himself. Both Schiller and the young Hegel believed that such a religion was immoral and self-contradictory, since true religion is, to use the young Hegel's terms, 'a free virtue springing from man's own being'. The passage from Schiller I am discussing also makes the point that man is led astray by his senses in believing the moral law to be 'something external to himself', the ordinance of a God also 'external to himself'. Man thus unwittingly enslaves himself to an idea of his own creation, which he has *objectified* into a powerful being whom he then proceeded to worship. Man invents his own God. We shall see this idea discussed and developed in the writings of the young Hegel. It is this very idea which Feuerbach, reacting as he believed against the Hegelian system, thought that he had discovered for himself when, in *The Essence of Christianity* (1841), he argued that it is man who invents God, that God is the alienated and externalized essence of man. This idea became one of the battlecries of the Young Hegelians, and in Marx's own writings came to be transformed into 'the fetishism of commodities' which in turn becomes one of the fundamental themes of Marxism.

Schiller's idea that man's lawgiver is not an external being but lies within himself he took from Kant (for whom his admiration was great). For Kant, true morality must be autonomous, self-legislated, and this self-legislation has also to be universal legislation. If it is not *both* autonomous and universal it is not morality. This, man comes to discover for himself at last; and for Schiller, Kant's *Critique of Practical Reason* (1788) articulated and buttressed with proofs what is an essential and fundamental feature of humanity. But for

Schiller this undoubted truth about the character of morality left man in a cleft stick. For it meant that man was perpetually divided between duty and inclination, between Reason and Nature, and not until this rift, the deepest and most fundamental of all, could be healed would man lead a life of happiness, at one with himself and with his fellow men.

> Reason is satisfied as long as her law obtains unconditionally. . . . Reason does indeed demand unity; but Nature demands multiplicity; and both these kinds of law make their claim upon man. The law of Reason is imprinted upon him by an incorruptible consciousness; the law of Nature by an ineradicable feeling. *Hence it will always argue a still defective education if the moral character is able to assert itself only by sacrificing the natural.* [But] a political constitution will still be very imperfect if it is able to achieve unity only by suppressing variety. The State should not only respect the objective and generic character in its individual subjects; it should also honour their subjective and specific character, and in extending the invisible realm of morals take care not to depopulate the sensible realm of appearance.[5]

Schiller also puts the problem in other words, which will clarify further the dilemma he puts before his readers and to resolve which he wrote his *Letters on the Aesthetic Education of Man*. He declares that if 'man is to retain his power of choice and yet, at the same time, be a reliable link in the chain of causality, this can only be brought about through both these motive forces, *inclination and duty*, producing completely identical results in the world of phenomena; . . . that is to say through *impulse* being sufficiently in harmony with *reason* to qualify as universal legislator'.[6] Man in the state of nature is an animal devoid of reason; man aware of the moral law is an animal endowed with reason. But man is meant to be neither: 'he is meant to be a human being. Nature is not meant to rule him exclusively, nor Reason to rule him conditionally. Both these systems of rule are meant to co-exist, in perfect independence of each other, *and yet in perfect concord*.'[7]

The healing of the rift in man, of the divisions between men, of the estrangement between mankind and nature, reconciliation, freedom, concord and harmony, this is Schiller's ideal – it is also Hegel's – and we may say that Hegel's whole philosophical endeavour is to find how, under modern conditions, 'man can experience a happy consciousness, how he can feel at home in the world'. This is what in his letter of 1800 to his friend Schelling he called 'the ideal of my youth'.

We can perhaps form a better understanding of this ideal if we attend to the way in which Schiller describes it. He puts before us a contrast between athletic bodies and beautiful ones. Athletic bodies can be developed by gymnastic exercises, 'beauty only through the free and harmonious play of the limbs. In the same way the keying up of individual functions of the mind can indeed produce extraordinary human beings; but only the equal tempering of them all, happy and complete human beings.'[8] The symbol for Schiller of this beautiful and harmonious life is the dance; in the dance, movement is at once spontaneous and governed by law. This law-governed spontaneity, this unceasing flow of dynamic form is the picture of a life which is free and harmonious, not anarchic and discordant. Here is his poem, *The Dance*, which so captivated Coleridge, in Bowring's Victorian translation:

> See! how they vanish from sight, in wild entanglement blended,
> Falls the edifice proud, built of this movable world.
> No, there it rises again exulting, the knot is unravell'd;

> While the old rule is restored, with but a new form of charm.
> Ever demolished, the whirling creation renews itself ever,
> And, by a law that is mute, each transformation is led.
> Say, how is it that, ever renewed the figures are hov'ring,
> While repose is not found, save in the changeable form?
> How is each one at freedom to follow the will of his bosom,
> And to find out the sole path, as he pursues his swift course?
> Wouldst thou know how it is? 'Tis Harmony's powerful Godhead,
> Changing the boisterous leap into the sociable dance,
> That, like Nemesis, links to the golden bridle of rhythm
> Every violent lust, taming each thing that was wild.

In the *Letters on the Aesthetic Education of Man* Schiller looks forward to the coming era of dynamic form:

> Removed alike from uniformity and from confusion, there abides the triumph of form. Wholeness of character must therefore be present in any people capable, and worthy, of exchanging a State of compulsion for a State of freedom.[9]

But as long as 'the split within man is not healed', and 'his nature restored to wholeness . . . every attempt at political reform will be untimely'. Only if wholeness is restored can man 'become the artificer of the State, and guarantee the reality of this political creation of Reason'.[10] If man 'is inwardly at one with himself, he will be able to preserve his individuality however much he may universalize his conduct, and the State will be merely the interpreter of his own finest instinct, a clearer formulation of what is right'.[11] Indeed, if the rift is healed and wholeness restored, Schiller says towards the end of his work, 'we shall see actual life governed by the ideal, honour triumphant over possessions, thought over enjoyment, dreams of immortality over existence. There public opinion will be the only thing to be feared, and an olive wreath bestow greater honour than a purple robe.'[12]

In Schiller's view such an ideal and aspiration is not a mere fantasy. For he believed that once, in the history of man, this ideal was a reality. This was in ancient Greece, and particularly in ancient Athens. There intellect was not sundered from sensibility, duty and inclination went hand in hand, and the state was indeed a State of freedom (*Staat der Freiheit*) and not a State of compulsion (*Staat der Not*). Our reputation for culture and refinement

> can avail us nothing against the natural humanity of the Greeks. For they were wedded to all the delights of art and all the dignity of wisdom, without however, like us, falling a prey to their seduction. The Greeks put us to shame not only by a simplicity to which our age is a stranger; they are at the same time our rivals, indeed often our models. . . . at once philosophic and creative, sensitive and energetic, the Greeks combined the first youth of imagination with the manhood of reason in a glorious manifestation of humanity.[13]

To use the title of Professor E. M. Butler's well-known work, Schiller's words exemplify *The Tyranny of Greece over Germany*. The word 'tyranny' is hardly an exaggeration for the powerful nostalgia which gripped so many of the greatest German writers at the end of the eighteenth century and the beginning of the nineteenth for a Greece and an Athens which seemed to be peopled not with men of flesh and blood – the men, say, portrayed in Thucydides with all their ruthlessness, their passion for power, their cruelty and lack of scruple – but with god-like beings; as though the Athenians were so many living and animated Apollos and Aphrodites.

## Hegel and Schiller

There is a famous poem by Schiller, *The Gods of Greece*, which gives powerful expression to this feeling of nostalgia and irreparable loss. Here are three stanzas, again I fear in Bowring's stilted translation:

> Gloomy sternness and denial sad
> Ne'er were in your service blest descried;
> Each heart throbbed then with emotions glad,
> For the Happy were with you allied.
> Nothing then was Holy, save the Fair;
> Of no rapture was the God asham'd,
> When the modest Man was blushing there, –
> When their sway the Graces claim'd!
> . . . . . . . . . . . . .
> Beauteous world, where art thou gone? Oh thou
> Nature's blooming youth, return once more!
> Ah, but in Song's fairy region now
> Lives thy fabled trace so dear of yore!
> Cold and perish'd, sorrow now the plains,
> Not one Godhead greets my longing sight
> Ah, the Shadow only now remains
> Of yon living Image bright!
> . . . . . . . . . . .

Nature now servilely obeys the law of gravitation 'her Godhead flown' and the poem ends:

> Aye! they honoured homeward go, – and they have
>     flown,
> All that's bright and fair they've taken too,
> Ev'ry colour, ev'ry living tone, -
> And a soulless world is all we view
> Borne off by the Time-flood's current strong,
> They on Pindus' height have safety found;
> All that is to live in endless song,
> Must in Life-time first be drowned!

In these concluding lines the nostalgia is so overpowering that we can say it amounts to a death-wish. Hölderlin, Hegel's close friend and exact contemporary for whom Schiller was a hero, was violently seized and mastered by this longing for a dead and imaginary world. From the year 1806 till he died in 1843 Hölderlin was patently out of his mind, and the symptoms of his madness had manifested themselves a few years earlier. It is perhaps not too much to say that Hölderlin's madness and his longing for this Greece of the imagination were intimately connected. Hegel's character was very different from that of his friend, and his admiration for the Greeks and for the life of the polis which *was* very strong did not lead him to madness. But for him, too, Greece remained the summit of human life. While rector of the gymnasium at Nürnberg, Hegel gave a speech at the end of the school year in 1809 on classical studies. He was then 39 years old. Of the ancients – and he had the Greeks principally in mind – he said that their world was 'the fairest that ever has been'. It was:

> the paradise of the human *spirit*, the paradise where the human spirit emerges like a bride from her chamber. . . . The human spirit manifests its profundity here no longer in confusion, gloom, or arrogance, but in perfect clarity. . . .
>
> The works of the ancients contain the most noble food in the most noble form: golden apples in silver bowls. They are incomparably richer than all the works of any other nation and of any other time. The greatness of their sentiments, their statuesque virtue free from moral ambiguity, their patriotism, the grand manner of their deeds and characters, the multiplicity of their destinies, of their morals and constitutions – to recall these is enough to vindicate the assertion that in the compass of no other civilization was there ever united so much that was splendid, admirable, original, many-sided, and instructive.[14]

So central is this admiration for Greece in Hegel that Professor Judith Shklar has called his political thought an elegy for Hellas. An elegy is a lament for something that is dead and gone for ever – and we may perhaps say that Hegel's political thought is an enquiry into the excellence of the Greek polis, into the reasons why it has disappeared and cannot possibly be revived in the modern world, and how that which existed in the polis, the feeling of wholeness, the absence of rift, division and estrangement, the being at home in the world, could be realized in a modern society so much larger and more complex than the simple 'polypoid' structure – to use Schiller's word – of the city-state.

For Schiller the Greek achievement is capable of being realized once again, and this by developing the aesthetic disposition in man. The aesthetic disposition does not relate to our sensual condition, to our intellect, or to our will: it is not physical, logical or moral. The aesthetic disposition is a disposition to contemplation with its aim as 'the development of the whole complex of our sensual and spiritual powers in the greatest possible harmony'. In the aesthetic state the psyche is free from compulsion, but not free from laws. But the laws that the free psyche follows are laws to be seen manifest in its spontaneous activity.[15] It is art and the contemplation of beauty which heals the rift; we attain truth through beauty; in a beautiful being, or a poem, or a piece of music, the finite and the infinite are fused, the sensuous and the intellectual, the physical and spiritual. Beauty alone can confer upon man a social character. 'Taste alone brings harmony into society, because it fosters harmony in the individual. All other forms of perception divide man, because they are founded exclusively either upon the sensuous or upon the spiritual part of his being; only the aesthetic mode of perception makes of him a whole, because both his natures must be in harmony if he is to achieve it.'[16] This, in bare summary, is Schiller's solution of the dilemma which led him to begin on the letters. It is not a solution which Hegel will consider at all adequate, although he fully agrees with Schiller's diagnosis of the predicament. But there is one statement in Schiller's last letter that has its reverberations in Hegel's thought. Schiller says that 'In the midst of the fearful kingdom of forces, and in the midst of the sacred kingdom of laws, the aesthetic impulse to form is at work, unnoticed, on the building of a third joyous kingdom of play and of semblance, in which man is relieved of the shackles of circumstance, and released from all that might be called constraint, alike in the physical and in the moral sphere.'

Thus, at the very end of his argument we see Schiller enter the realm of history. There are, unbeknown to us, forces at work, Schiller tells us, which will inaugurate the third joyous kingdom in which all constraint has disappeared. The expectation of such a third kingdom is expressed, however, much more eloquently, and argued for much more cogently in the writings of another author whose influence over Hegel's thought was fundamental – G. E. Lessing.

## Notes

1 Letter 6, p. 33, p. 35.
2 Third letter, paras 1–2, p. 11.
3 Letter 24, para 7, p. 179.
4 *Early Theological Writings: G. W. F. Hegel*, ed. T. M. Knox and Richard Kroner (Philadelphia, University of Pennsylvania Press, 1981), p. 71.
5 Letter 4, para 3, p. 19.
6 Letter 4, para 1, p. 17.
7 Letter 24, para 8, p. 181.
8 Letter 6, para 14, p. 43.
9 Letter 4, para 7, p. 23.
10 Letter 7, para 1, p. 45.
11 Letter 4, para 5, p. 21.
12 Letter 26, para 12, p. 199.

13 Letter 6, para 2, p. 31.
14 Knox and Kroner, pp. 325–6.
15 Letter 20, para 4, p. 141.
16 Letter 27, para 10, p. 215.

# 4
# HEGEL AND LESSING

I ended my last lecture with a quotation from the last of Schiller's *Letters on the Aesthetic Education of Man*, where Schiller declares that:

> in the midst of the fearful kingdom of forces, and in the midst of the sacred kingdom of laws, the aesthetic impulse to form is at work, unnoticed, on the building of a third joyous kingdom of play and of semblance, in which man is relieved of the shackles of circumstance, and released from all that might be called constraint, alike in the physical and in the moral sphere.

(By 'kingdom of forces' Schiller meant physical nature and its laws ascertained by science, and by 'kingdom of laws' he meant the laws of morality decreed by the categorical imperative as expounded by Kant.)

In this passage Schiller is looking forward to an era in which humanity would be free from the rift in the soul, from social division and from the political oppression which is its concomitant. This will be the third kingdom, a 'joyous' kingdom, to establish which all human history is tending. Though men immersed in their own immediate environment cannot know this, yet human history is working in all kinds of indirect and unexpected ways towards such a terminus or, to use stronger words, towards such a consummation, or even (we can say) towards such a transfiguration.

In speaking like this, Schiller was not indulging in loose or flamboyant or meaningless rhetoric. To himself, and to his educated audience, the expression 'third kingdom' would have evoked a precise doctrine, a distinct philosophy of history – to use a term which by the time Schiller published his *Letters* had become familiar to the educated classes of Europe. It is particularly pertinent to our purpose here to note that references to a similar order of ideas occur in a short work, quite as influential and important as Schiller's *Letters*, which was published by G. E. Lessing in 1780, a year before his death, when Hegel was ten years old. This work, too, had the word 'education' in its title. The work I am referring to is *The Education of the Human Race*.

It is beyond any doubt and attested by much evidence that Hegel and his circle, and in particular Schelling and Hölderlin, were closely acquainted with Lessing's writings and ideas. In a letter of 1795 Schelling called Hegel 'a familiar of Lessing's'. The term is not an exaggeration, because since he was a schoolboy (as we know from compositions of his which have survived) Hegel was very much attracted by Lessing, and I want now to consider briefly some of his ideas which are particularly relevant to this enquiry. One of Lessing's works with which Hegel was closely acquainted from his schoolboy days was the play *Nathan the Wise* which Lessing published in 1779 – one year before *The Education of the Human Race*. Some of the themes of the play recur in the later work, and in fact had been at the centre of Lessing's thought for many years before. Nathan is not so much a play for the stage as a drama of ideas. Its hero, Nathan, is a Jewish merchant living in the Jerusalem which Saladin had reconquered from the Crusaders. Lessing portrays Nathan – who is supposed to have been modelled on his intimate friend Moses

Mendelssohn, the Berlin philosopher – as a man of great nobility of character and deep wisdom. The centrepiece of the play is a scene in which Saladin, having summoned the merchant before him, demands to be told what Nathan (whom the people nicknamed 'the wise') considers to be the best religion. Nathan is taken aback. Sultan, he says, I am a Jew. And I am a Muslim, replies Saladin. Between us there is a Christian. Of these three religions surely one must be the true one. What does Nathan think? In order to answer the Sultan, Nathan makes use of a parable which he takes from a fable by Boccaccio. Long ago an Oriental had a wonderful ring of opal which had the power of making acceptable in God's and men's sight anyone who wore it in this faith. The owner constantly kept it on his finger and was resolved to keep it forever in his family. He bequeathed the ring to the son whom he most loved and ordered that the son should do the same. The holder of this ring, regardless of primogeniture, would become the head of his house. The ring at last descended to the father of three sons. These three were so good and obedient that the father loved them all equally. To whom was he to bequeath the ring? He adopts a stratagem. He gets a craftsman to make two more rings which would be identical with the original. The craftsman was so skilled that the owner of the ring himself when the rings were brought back to him was unable to distinguish the original from the copies. The father sees each son privately and gives him his blessing and his ring. Shortly afterwards he dies, and each of the three sons exhibits his ring and claims that he is entitled to be the head of the family. Investigations, quarrels and mutual accusations ensue, but it was impossible to prove who had the true ring, 'Almost as impossible', says Nathan, 'as it is for us to prove what is the true faith.' To continue with the story, the three brothers submit their quarrel to a judge. The judge declares that a decision was clearly impossible without the evidence of their father, and this was obviously unobtainable. There was, however, one fact which might help to solve the dispute. The original ring had the magic virtue of attracting God's love to its wearer and making him in turn love God and his fellows. To whom among you three is this applicable? Obviously to none since you are all three quarrelling among you. Can the answer be that your father lost the original ring, and that to conceal the loss he had three identical – but counterfeit – rings made? Or is it that your father intended each one of you to consider his ring as the true one? Perhaps your father had decided no longer to tolerate in his house the tyranny of one ring? What is clear is that he loved you all three equally since he decided not to bestow his gift on only one among you. If each one of you were to strive by his behaviour to make active the power of the opal, by his tolerance, by his good works, by his obedience to God, then the virtue of the ring will manifest itself in your descendants. I will summon you to appear before this court in a thousand years' time, and then one who is wiser than me will sit in judgement and pronounce sentence.

The parable is transparent enough. The three rings are the three religions, Judaism, Christianity and Islam, and their worth and truth depends on the behaviour of their respective followers. All three are facets of a single truth. But like all good parables, this one too has the necessary element of ambiguity. The three rings, are they genuine or counterfeit? The three religions, are they facets of the truth or superstitions masking the truth? We may think that this ambiguity about revealed scriptural religions was something which Lessing intended. For *Nathan the Wise* followed some four years of sometimes bitter ideological controversies in which Lessing was involved. The involvement came about in this way. In the course of his career, Lessing came to be employed as the resident critic of the Hamburg Municipal Theatre (and produced in the process a body of criticism collected under the title *Hamburgische Dramaturgie*, which had a far-reaching effect on German literary theory and practice). While there, he became friendly with a professor of Oriental Languages at Hamburg, Hermann Samuel Reimarus (1694–1768). Reimarus was a believer in rational – as against revealed – religion and his published writings were a defence of the truth of natural religion. But his *magnum opus* was a manuscript 4,000 pages long which he did not dare to publish, but which circulated anonymously among his friends. The manuscript, entitled 'An Apology for the Rational Worshippers of God', was a radical and severe critique of the biblical narratives and the historical claims of Christianity. Between 1774 and 1778 Lessing published six extracts from this manuscript accompanied by a commentary. In publishing what are called the Wolfenbüttel Fragments Lessing did not disclose the name of the author, but claimed that they were from an unknown author whose manuscript he had found in the library of the Duke of Brunswick at Wolfenbüttel, where he had been appointed librarian. The titles of two of the fragments will indicate the drift of the argument: the second fragment was entitled 'The Impossibility of a Revelation which all Men can believe on Grounds of Reason', and the fifth was entitled 'On the Accounts of the Resurrection'. Reimarus argued in these fragments that however convincing a revelation might be to those who first received it, it could never be a subject of rational religious belief to others who had to take it from tradition or documentary evidence. Consider the scriptural accounts of the Resurrection: they were hopelessly riddled with discrepancies and no believer who relied on the scripture could give an incontrovertible account of this central episode of Christianity. The sixth fragment, entitled 'The Aim of Jesus and his Disciples' argued that the aims of Jesus were political. His ambition was to re-establish David's kingdom. This was the meaning of his claim to be the Messiah, and it was so understood by his followers and by the Roman authorities who put him to death. After his crucifixion his disciples were shocked and disappointed, and fell back on the idea of a supernatural Messiah. It was thus that they invented the story of the resurrection of Jesus, and, invented as it was, the story was naturally riddled with all kinds of contradictions and implausibilities.

The Wolfenbüttel Fragments aroused, quite naturally, great anger, and Lessing was bitterly attacked by many clerical writers. We may then perhaps see that *Nathan* was Lessing's retort to his attackers. The exclusive claims of Judaism, Christianity and Islam were all of them false and untenable, and what truth there was in them was the truth derived from the one true religion – the original opal ring – a religion the tenets of which are now buried under thick layers of superstition and deceit. But what was this true religion? A character in one of Disraeli's novels claims that all sensible men are of one religion, but what this religion was sensible men never tell. With the first part of the statement Lessing, to judge by his published religious beliefs, would have agreed, but his published writings also show that he did not altogether agree with the second part. For he was willing and ready publicly to disclose if not the whole truth, then a good part of the truth about it. This is clear from what he makes Nathan say to Saladin, and also from his five Masonic dialogues, *Ernst und Falk*, the first three of which he published in 1778 (and the last two in 1780). Ernst is an earnest enquirer after the truth, and he seeks illumination from his friend, the Freemason Falk; illumination about the hidden truth which Freemasons are supposed to possess and to communicate only to those who are admitted to their society. By dint of questioning, Ernst ascertains from Falk that Freemasons form an invisible church, the members of which give themselves the task of bringing together men who are alienated from one another – alienated by differences of religion, of language and culture, and of economic interests. These divisions have come about, Falk observes, not because men are bad and malevolent, but precisely as a result of their benevolent and gregarious instincts. These instincts lead them to gather together in societies and states in order the better to secure their share of happiness. It is this very process which ends by engendering social, economic and political divisions and antagonisms. Freemasons, Falk affirms, have accomplished all that is good in the world, but their actions are not easily detected. Many centuries will pass before people are able to point to these actions. The actions have a single aim, namely to render superfluous most of the things that are today called good actions. By these enigmatic words Lessing no doubt means that the activity of the Freemasons will eventually abolish all divisions and antagonisms between human beings, that men will be naturally and instinctively friendly towards one another in a way such that there will be no need for anyone to take action in order to reconcile antagonisms or to heal divisions. We may note here a passage which occurs in a letter of 1795 from Hegel to Schelling in which Hegel says: 'Reason and Freedom remain our watchword, and our rallying point the invisible Church.' And we may also note a passage in a letter two years earlier from Hölderlin to a younger half-brother in which he declares:

> I love the race of the coming centuries. For this is my most sacred hope . . . that our descendants will be better than we, that freedom must sometimes come to pass,

and that virtue will flourish better in the holy light of warmth and freedom.... We are living in a period when everything works together towards better days. The seeds of enlightenment, the silent wishes and stirrings of individuals towards the formulation of the human race will spread and grow stronger, and bear noble fruits.

Hegel's reference to the invisible church in which the watchword is Reason and Freedom, and Hölderlin's anticipation of 'better days' to be achieved through 'the silent wishes and strivings of individuals towards the formation of the human race', his looking forward to the era when 'the holy light of warmth and freedom' will envelop all human life, are so many significant indications that what we have here is a theology and a philosophy of history which is disaffected towards the orthodox traditional teaching of the Stift, the 'old sourdough' as Hegel so expressively put it. Hegel, as we shall see, had no use for traditional Christian theology, entertained indeed a great antipathy to the organized Christian churches – whether Catholic or Protestant. But the advent of the third kingdom was not a simple matter of the children of light overthrowing the children of darkness. The philosophy of history to be found in Lessing cautioned against that. We have already seen this from a consideration of *Nathan* and of *Ernst und Falk*. In *Nathan*, the three religions may be superstitions, but, on the other hand, they may be aspects, albeit fragmentary and limited, of the truth. There is undoubted ambiguity here. Again, in *Ernst und Falk* Lessing argues that it is men's search for a satisfactory social life which engenders division and antagonism. In this argument we have the sketch of a dialectical view of history, a view according to which historical change is the outcome of the unintended consequences of men's actions. A view which, as we have seen, is hinted at by Schiller's language in the passage about the third kingdom. What is hinted at and imperfectly worked out elsewhere, we see argued incisively in *The Education of the Human Race*.

In the preface to this work – composed of 100 short paragraphs – Lessing boldly asks: 'Why should we not in all positive Religions see nothing other than the order in which the human understanding everywhere *solely and by itself* is developed and must continue to develop . . . ?' Human history is the history of the human mind gradually coming to full self-possession. What education is to the individual, Lessing declares in his first paragraph, revelation is to the whole human race.

Thus in paragraph 2: 'Revelation is education, which has been, and *is still being imparted* to the human race.' Paragraph 4 continues: 'Education gives to the individual *nothing* which he could not attain by his own efforts.' However, education gives it more quickly and easily. 'Revelation imparts to the human race nothing which the human understanding, *if left to itself*, could not also discover.' But revelation gives it sooner. Revelation could not come about all at once, Lessing hints in his fifth paragraph: 'God had to observe, in his revelation a certain order, a certain measure' – as in education.

God chose a single people for his education, 'the most uncivilized, the most degenerate people that He might begin with at the very beginning.'[1]

He familiarized them with the idea of divine unity. In due course, by means of their exile in Babylon, God familiarized the Jews, by putting them in contact with 'the wise Persian', with the idea of God as the God of the whole universe.[2]

'Thus enlightened upon their own unrecognized treasures, they returned and became an entirely different people, whose first care it was to make this enlightenment a lasting one among themselves.'[3]

They were taught the immortality of the soul by contact with Greek thought.[4] The idea was there in their sacred writings, but as hints, allusions and a preparatory discipline.

A better teacher, a more advanced teacher came – Jesus – whose mission it was 'to enjoin an inner purity of heart in view of a future life'.[5]

His disciples spread his teaching to the whole world. A new era is arriving in which truths foreshadowed in revelation will become clear to the understanding.[6] What these truths are I shall come back to.

Lessing then proceeds to prophesy the next stage in the progress of the human race, the end to which all education has tended: 'It will come, it will certainly come, the time of consummation when man, however firmly his mind is convinced of an ever better future, yet will have no need to borrow motives for his conduct from that future. For he will do right because it is right, and not because arbitrary rewards are attached to it.'[7]

In paragraph 86, Lessing says that it will certainly come, the time of this *new eternal gospel*, which is promised us already in the elementary books of the New Covenant.[8]

In paragraph 87 he argues that it may indeed be that certain visionaries had already in the thirteenth and fourteenth centuries caught a glimpse of this new eternal gospel, and that their error merely lay in predicting for it so speedy an advent.[9]

'It may be that their *threefold age of the world* was not by any means an idle fancy; and it was assuredly with no evil purpose that they taught that the New Covenant must become *antiquated*, as the Old Covenant had already done.'[10]

'But they hastened it too much, believing that they could, at one stroke, without enlightenment, without preparation, change their contemporaries, who had scarcely outgrown their infancy, into men worthy of their *third age*.'[11]

The *Education of the Human Race* was, as I have said, published in 1780; that is, nine years before the outbreak of the French Revolution, and if we are to appreciate the impact it made on such young readers as Hegel, Hölderlin and Schelling, we must bring to our minds the probability that the third age it heralded must have seemed to them, with so much hopeful change around them, to be on the point of being inaugurated. But whether such hopes were destined to be fulfilled or disappointed – and they were disappointed – there remained as their residue the vivid sense that history has a sense, a direction, a terminus, that it was not the inert and dead thing that the pious orthodoxies by which they were surrounded made it out to be, that it had a life of its own, an autonomous movement and logic, and that they themselves were living at one particular hinge, a decisive turning-point in this history. Lessing taught them that like morality, history was autonomous, that man collectively makes himself. Marxism is very frequently proclaimed to be a humanism, and if by humanism we mean the belief that man's achievements and predicaments are of his own making, then this Marxist humanism surely has its roots here; it is from this teaching, transmitted via Hegel and Feuerbach, that it is derived. For Lessing's education of the human race is an uncompromisingly secular education. For him revelation is merely a crash course in history. Revelation, as he says at the very outset of his work, imparts to the human race nothing which the human understanding, *if* left to *itself*, could not also discover.

Lessing's teaching has yet one other feature which was to prove of enormous importance in Hegel's thinking, which I will proceed to examine.

## Notes

1 Lessing, *Die Erziehung des Menschengeschlechts* (Berlin, 1780) [*The Education of the Human Race*, contained in *The Laocoon and Other Prose Writings of Lessing*, trans. and ed. W. B. Rönnfeldt, London, Walter Scott Ltd. 1895], para 8.
2 Ibid., para 39.
3 Ibid., para 40.
4 Ibid., paras 42–46.
5 Ibid., para 61.
6 Ibid., para 72.
7 Ibid., para 85.
8 Revelation of St. John the Divine, 14: 6.
9 Joachim of Flora, *c*.1130–1202, Gerard of Borgo San Donnino *Introductorium in Evangelium Aeternum*, 1254.
10 Lessing, *The Education of the Human Race*, para 88. Period of law, of grace, of love. Father; son; spirit, power and dread; humility, truth and wisdom; love. Revelation 21: 1: 'And I saw a new heaven and a new earth.'
11 Lessing, *The Education of the Human Race*, para 89.

# 5
# 'ONE AND ALL'

History has a meaning and a direction, and the third age will come, will certainly come, Lessing affirms. 'Advance at thy imperceptible pace, eternal Providence! But let me not, because it is imperceptible, despair of thee.'[1] Providence, Lessing also tells us, advances not only imperceptibly, but also in such a manner that the advance seems to our eyes a backward step. And here Lessing introduces a powerful and vivid image not so much to explain as to convey imaginatively his meaning. 'What', he asks, 'if it were as good as proved that that great, slowly turning wheel, which carries the race nearer to its perfection, is set in motion only by smaller and quicker wheels, each of which revolves for that very purpose?'[2] In fact it could not be otherwise, and the groove which leads the great wheel to the third age of perfection must itself be traversed by each of the small wheels which impel the great wheel along. The small wheels represent individual human beings, and the question therefore arises whether the history of humanity is duplicated in the biography of every individual. Would this be possible in a single lifetime? Obviously not. Lessing's answer to this objection is: 'Why may not each individual human being have existed more than once in this world?'[3] Does Lessing, then, believe in the transmigration of souls, and in some form perhaps of eternal recurrence? Why not? he says. The theory is the oldest such, but is this a reason for dismissing it? 'Why may I not return again as often as it is possible for one to acquire new knowledge, new skill? Do I carry so much away with me *at one time* as to render my return useless?'[4] Or is the objection that 'too much time would thus be lost to me? Lost? And what, then, have I to lose? Is not the wheel of Eternity mine?'[5] With this enigmatic, not to say mysterious, paragraph, ends Lessing's meditation on the education of the human race. What could he have meant by it? The reader of Lessing's masterpiece – for it surely is a masterpiece – finds himself in the space of 100 short paragraphs transported a very great distance indeed. The work begins with revelation. Revelation implies a God who vouchsafes it to mankind, that is, to finite beings whom he has created. It ends by suggesting that the life of these individuals is eternal, and so therefore not finite. How does Lessing resolve this paradox? He does it by an argument which tends to show that between the finite and the infinite the gap is not so great as is commonly thought; that in fact there is no gap at all between them; that the finite partakes of the infinite, and the infinite bodies forth the finite. Lessing does this in a group of paragraphs (73–5) which are the longest, most difficult and most ambiguous in the whole work. In paragraph 72, Lessing declares that just as we no longer require the Old Testament to convince ourselves of the unity of God so now we do not require the New Testament to believe in the immortality of the soul. This is because the human race, now more mature, has outgrown the elementary schoolbooks which are suitable for children. But the human race has not stopped growing in maturity and wisdom. Might not the truths foreshadowed, hinted at, in the New Testament, be now more clearly grasped as philosophical truths, rather than be merely apprehended in a symbolic or imaginative form?

What are these truths? For example, take the doctrine of the Trinity. The doctrine is one of the mysteries of the Christian religion, which men have so far accepted on authority rather than understood rationally. Lessing proceeds to suggest the true rational, philosophical meaning of the doctrine. And if this meaning is once grasped, then the manner in which it is expressed in the traditional Christian creeds will be seen to be needlessly mystificatory. Can it be, Lessing asks, that the doctrine of the Trinity is meant to intimate to us that God cannot possibly be *One*, in the sense that ordinary things are One, that 'His unity must be a transcendental Unity, which does not exclude a kind of plurality.' How may this be established? God, we must assume, is perfect, by definition. If he is perfect, then it follows that he has the most perfect conception of himself. This means a conception which includes all that is within himself. But such a conception cannot be merely a conception, that is, merely 'a possibility of His necessary reality', for mere possibility does not exhaust reality. *Therefore* either God's perfect conception of all that is within himself must be as real as God himself (that is, it cannot be mere possibility), or God cannot have a perfect conception of himself, which by definition is impossible, therefore QED. The syllogism is all very well, but what in fact are its substantive implications? Lessing here has recourse to an image in order to put across the daring thought to which he has been leading up. 'My reflection in a mirror is indeed', he says, 'nothing more than an empty *conception* or representation of myself; for it only contains that part of me from which the light falls on [the mirror's] surface. *But* if this reflection contained *everything*, without exception, that forms part of myself, would it still be nothing more than an empty representation? Would it not rather be a true duplication of myself?' Lessing hints it is the same with God.

There is a similar duplication of God. The duplication is of all that is contained within God, a duplication not of possibilities but of realities. What is it which fits this specification? It is the universe. The universe is the duplicate of God, is God, in the same way that the image in the mirror is I myself. This is the rational, philosophical meaning of the Christian creed which is imaginatively expressed by saying that God has a *Son* whom he has begotten from eternity. The world is God, and God is the world and all that happens, has happened and will happen in it.

Paragraph 75 gives a similar 'philosophical' account of the Christian creed concerning the Atonement of the Son. This creed really means, according to Lessing, that God chose to forgive man all his transgressions in consideration of his *Son* – 'i.e.,' Lessing explains, 'in consideration of the self-contained extent of all His perfections, against and in which every imperfection of the individual disappears'. What Lessing is hinting at here is that all imperfection, all lack, all division, all limitation, all evil in the world is a part, a necessary part, the warp – complementing the woof in the world's perfect fabric – perfect because it is the duplication of God, is God.

The vision of which Lessing seeks to persuade us in these short and allusive passages is one of the small number of genuine metaphysical – or, if you prefer, religious – visions which man has conceived. It is a vision of everything, man included, a part of one great eternal enfolding Whole. It may help us to grasp the character of this vision if we were to examine notable expressions of it which occur in imaginative literature. Here are three examples, the first of which is a meditation on life and death:

> Once here, the future is an idleness,
> The clear-cut insect scratches at the dryness;

> Everything's burned, dispelled, received in air
> Into I know not what impartial essence. . . .
> Life is immense, being drunk with its own absence,
> And bitterness is sweet, the mind clear.
> . . . . . . . . . . . . . . . . . . . . .
> And Noon up there, Noon the motionless,
> Thinks its own thought approving its own self. . . .
> Total head, and perfect diadem,
> I am the secret changing in your mind.
>
> I am all you have to contain your fears!
> My doubts, my strivings, my repentances,
> These are the flaw in your great diamond. . . .
> But in their darkness under a marble load
> An empty people among the tree roots
> Have gradually come to take your side.
>
> They have melted into a dense unbeing,
> The red clay has drained the paler kind,
> The gift of living has passed into flowers!
> . . . . . . . . . . . . . . . . . . . . .
> All goes to earth and back into the game!
>   (Valéry, *The Graveyard by the Sea*, translated by
>   David Paul)

The second, from Eliot's *Little Gidding*, shows Hegelian ideas mediated to the poet through Bradley:

> And all shall be well and
> All manner of thing shall be well
> When the tongues of flame are in-folded
> Into the crowned knot of fire
> And the fire and the rose are one.

The last is a passage by Emerson. It is the most explicit, but not in the same class as Eliot or Valéry:

> If the red slayer think he slays,
> Or if the slain think he is slain,
> They know not well the subtle ways
> I keep, and pass, and turn again.

> Far or forgot to me is near;
> Shadow and sunlight are the same;
> The vanished gods to me appear
> And to me are shame and fame.
> They reckon ill who leave me out;
> When me they fly, I am the wings;
> I am the doubter and the doubt,
> And I the hymn the Brahmin sings.

Emerson's poem is entitled 'Brahma'. The metaphysical vision it tries to convey is the vision of what has been called non-theistic religions – religions like Hinduism or Buddhism. Though this vision has also at times been that of Christian and Muslim mystics (witness the passage from Eliot's poem, and Eliot was a member of the Church of England), yet by and large such a vision belongs at the opposite end to that associated with theistic religions. In the philosophical and religious controversies of Christian Europe the vision conveyed by these poems (and by Lessing) has been described (and condemned) as pantheism, the belief that God is fully immanent in and in no way distinct from the world. We may say that it is of such a vision that Lessing – for all his talk of revelation and scriptures and so on – wishes to persuade his readers. To someone who believed in the orthodox tenets of Christianity, such a vision was tantamount to atheism. Tantamount to atheism because such a vision dismisses out of court the idea of a personal God who rules the world he has created, and who is clearly to be distinguished from his creation. It is because he was supposed to hold views which would have to lead to such a conclusion that Spinoza was denounced. And it is the case that Spinoza held that God was infinite substance, absolute, spontaneous, self-creating (*Deus sive natura, natura naturans, natura naturata*). However circumspect Lessing was in his public pronouncements on such issues – and we have seen that the *Education of the Human Race* is ambiguous and enigmatic – yet in private he left no doubt where he stood. Four years after his death, in 1785, a friend of his, F. H. Jacobi, published a work entitled *Letters to Moses Mendelssohn on the Teaching of Spinoza*. It had come to Jacobi's knowledge that Mendelssohn was preparing a work on Lessing who had been his intimate friend. Jacobi wrote to ask whether Mendelssohn knew that Lessing had been a Spinozist. Mendelssohn was shocked by what he considered to be a scandalous and baseless accusation against his friend, and asked Jacobi what proof he had of his allegations. Jacobi wrote back at great length, and eventually, two years later, published his letters. In these letters he began by recounting how in the summer of 1780, shortly before Lessing's death, he had gone to stay with him at Wolfenbüttel, and how one morning, he, Jacobi, showed him a poem by Goethe (who was himself a long-standing friend of Jacobi's) which he considered to express unorthodox and daring ideas about God and man's attitude to him. Lessing read the poem and said he did not find it in the least bit scandalous. He himself had entertained such ideas for a long time. He continued, 'The point of view which is at the origin of this poem, is itself my own point of view. Orthodox ideas of the divine are no longer for me. I cannot appreciate them, *en kai pan*! I know nothing else.'[6] Jacobi asked whether Lessing was therefore in agreement with Spinoza. Lessing replied: 'If I am to be called after anyone, I know nobody else [after whom I should be called].' During this visit, Jacobi and Lessing had further long conversations which Jacobi recounts in great detail, the upshot of which was to establish beyond any doubt that Lessing's idea of God was that he was the all-embracing reality, and that nothing which existed could be understood apart from God. In the course of one such conversation, Lessing went so far as to say with a smile that he himself was perhaps the supreme being, now, however, in a state of extreme contraction.[7]

Goethe's poem, which Jacobi showed Lessing and which precipitated his confession that his religion was that of the *en kai pan*, was called 'Prometheus'. In it Prometheus addresses to Zeus a defiant challenge. Zeus may try his strength on trees and on mountains, 'but you will have to leave me my earth, my cottage which you have not built, and my hearth the fire in which you covet'. Gods, Prometheus says, are of no help to man. It was your own heart, he says, addressing himself, which has defended you against the arrogance of the Titans, and saved you from death and slavery, and all the while, being blind, you were addressing your thanksgiving to 'the Sleeper, up above'. It was not Zeus who has made Prometheus into a man 'but all-powerful Time and eternal Fate, my masters and yours'. 'Here I am,' the poem ends, 'I knead men in my image, a race similar to myself, which will suffer and weep, taste and enjoy pleasure, and despise you as I do.' Goethe's poem enables us to situate Lessing's Spinozism more precisely. It is not a calm, passive contemplation of the universe which is divine, and of which man is part. Time and fate, it is true, are his masters, but man all the same is active, a doer who by no means abandons himself to the flow of time, or to fate's decree. He makes or modifies the world of which he is a part. If the world is God, then man, being part of it, is Godlike. The human race is educated by its own efforts into an ever-increasing understanding of, and harmony with, the active forces of the universe, into becoming more and more divine. Marxism, as I have said earlier, has been called a humanism; it has also been frequently described as Promethean. Like its humanism, the Promethean character of Marxism has its roots in the aspirations and speculations of those whom Hegel and his friends looked upon as their mentors. For there is absolutely no doubt that they looked upon Lessing as their mentor, and equally no doubt that the secret which Jacobi revealed in his *Letters on the Teaching of Spinoza* made a tremendous impression on them. We know that Jacobi's book was among the works which were read in Hegel's circle at the Stift. About 1790 Hölderlin acquired the symbol *en kai pan*, copying in a notebook the passage from Jacobi in which Lessing said that he knew no other religion than *en kai pan*. In the following year, 1791, Hölderlin and other friends each wrote an inscription in an album of Hegel's on the occasion of his going home for a vacation. Hölderlin's inscription consisted of two lines of a poem of Goethe's, also 'Promethean' in tendency.

> Desire and Love are the wings
> [carrying us] to great deeds.
> [Lust und Liebe sind
> die Fittige zu großen Taten.]

To this, someone, perhaps Hölderlin, perhaps Hegel himself, later added in a different pen with a different ink the symbol *en kai pan*.

What did Hegel, Hölderlin and their circle understand by the religion of *en kai pan*, of the One-and-All, and what was its significance for them? Perhaps the best way of elucidating this is by looking at a work of Hölderlin's, *Hyperion or the Hermit in Greece*, a novel written in a series of letters sent by the Greek Hyperion to his friend Bellarmin, describing his upbringing in Smyrna, his political and moral education, his love for Diotima, his disastrous participation in the abortive Greek uprising against the Ottomans in 1770, his exile in Germany, and his return to the Greek islands where he was leading the life of a hermit, all passion spent. Hölderlin was busy on the work at the time when both he and Hegel were at

Frankfurt, and it was in fact published in two instalments in 1797 and 1799. The work is powerfully evocative of the mood and emotions which were associated, in Hölderlin and his friends, with the idea of the union of the one and the all, the new religion which was to restore freedom and harmony to a world in which everything was rift, division, estrangement. About this estranged, alien, modern world Hölderlin says, in a fragment called 'New World': 'And the sky hangs, like an iron arch, above us, a curse paralyses the limbs of men, the gladdening gifts of Earth are like chaff, the Mother mocks us with her gifts and everything is unreal.' And in one of his great poems, *The Archipelago* (1800):

But woe! now our people strays in long night, as in Orcus[8]
Dwells without the divine. Each man is forged to his labour,
Only his own, and in the workshop's uproar
Hears only himself; and greatly the savages toil,
With powerful arms, and restless, yet ever and ever
Infertile as the Furies the wretches' efforts remain . . . [9]

In *Hyperion* we find set against this rift and desolation afflicting modern man the vision of a new world, a new church, a new man who shall renew 'the terrifying splendour of Antiquity' by which Hyperion declares himself to have been seized. *Hyperion* indeed combines in its brief compass the themes of Schiller's *Aesthetic Education* and Lessing's *Education of Mankind*. Thus Hyperion describes in very unflattering terms the condition of the modern Germans; they are 'Barbarians from the remotest past, whom industry and science and even religion have made yet more barbarous, profoundly incapable of any divine emotion, disqualified to the marrow for the delights of the sacred graces, offensive to every well-conditioned soul'. There is 'no people more at odds with themselves than the Germans. You see artisans but no men, thinkers but no men, priests but no men, masters and servants but no men, minors and adults but no men. . . . The virtues of the Germans are glittering vices and no more. . . . I tell you: there is nothing sacred that is not desecrated, is not debased to a miserable expedient among this people.'[10] Why is the German like this? Because 'In the North one must be judicious before one's capacity for feeling has fully developed . . . the oneness of the whole man, Beauty, is not allowed to thrive and ripen in him. . . . Pure intellect, pure reason are always the Kings of the North.'[11]

The East is no better. The Egyptian likewise is an incomplete being. Before he has 'learned to walk he is forced to kneel, before he has learned to speak, he is forced to pray . . . The dumb dark Isis is his first and last, an empty infinity, and out of that nothing reasonable has ever come.' Only the Greek is the complete man: 'He who does not live loving Heaven and Earth and loved by them in equal measure, he who does not live at one with the element in which he has his being, is by his very nature not so at one with himself as a Greek.' To be at one with the universe, and at one with oneself, *en kai pan*, is the great theme of Hyperion.[12]

> To be one with all – this is the life divine, this is man's heaven.[13] . . .
>
> The great saying . . . *the one differentiated in itself* of Hevaelitus . . . is the very being of Beauty, and before that was found there was no philosophy.[14] . . .
>
> There will be but one Beauty; and man and nature will be united in one all-embracing divinity.[15] . . .
>
> What would this world itself be, if it were not a harmony of free beings?
>
> . . . because I feel that I am free in the highest sense, that I have no beginning, therefore I believe that I shall have no end. But I am indestructible. If a potter's hand

made me, he may smash his vessel whenever he pleases. But what lives must be unbegotten, must be of divine nature in its seed, raised above all force and all art, and therefore inviolable, eternal.[16] . . .

We represent perfection in mutability; we divide the great harmonies of joy into changing melodies. . . . we live, ourselves divine, among the quiet Gods of the World, with our fleeting lovesong we temper the blissful seriousness of the Sun God and the rest.[17] . . .

I have felt the life of Nature, which is higher than all thought – if I become a plant would that be so great a loss? . . . How should I be lost from the sphere of life, in which eternal love, common to all, holds all natures together? how should I escape from the union that binds all beings together?[18] . . .

Like lovers' quarrels are the dissonances of the world. Reconciliation is there, in the midst of strife, and all things that are parted find one another again.

The arteries separate and return to the heart and all is one eternal glowing life.[19]

But when, to use Eliot's image, will the fire and the rose be one? In Eliot's case it can be at any time in any place, for his is a vision of the union of the individual soul with God and when it happens then it will be in a time not in time and in a place which is in no place. Not so with Hyperion.

Love brought to birth millenniums filled with living men; friendship will give birth to them again. Once upon a time the peoples set forth from the harmony of childhood; the harmony of spirits will be the beginning of another history of man. . . . By this, by this ideal, this rejuvenated divinity, the few recognize one another and are one, for one thing is in them; and from them, from them, the world's second age begins.[20] . . .

Do you ask me when this will be? It will be when the darling of Time, the youngest loveliest daughter of Time, the new Church, will arise out of these polluted antiquated forms.[21] . . .

> The new union of spirits cannot live in the air, the sacred theocracy of the Beautiful must dwell in a free state, and that state must have a place on earth, and that place we shall surely conquer.[22]

This is what Hyperion tells his beloved Diotima. For Hölderlin then, in this mood, the religion of *en kai pan* is an optimistic and activist religion. What has been once, must be again, and *we* will bring it about. But Hölderlin was subject also to another, later mood which we should also perhaps notice. It is best expressed in a later work, *Bread and Wine*, one of his greatest poems, and a powerful poem indeed. The poem is an elegy for the departed gods of Greece, who have gone leaving men alone and forsaken:

> ... where are they? the flowers, the familiar the crowns
>     of the feast-day?
> Thebes and Athens wilt, do, then, the weapons no more
> Sound in Olympia, nor yet the golden chariots of
>     combat,
> And no longer do wreaths deck the Corinthian ships?
> . . . . . . . . . . . . . . .
> But, my friend, we have come too late. True the gods are
>     living,
> But over our heads, above in a different world ...
> Endlessly there they act and – see how the heavenly
>     spare us! -
> Care very little, it seems, whether or not we exist.
> . . . . . . . . . . . . . . .
> Only a dream about them is life henceforth.
> . . . . . . . . . . . . . . .
> Then as a sign that they had once been here and again
>     would
> Come, the heavenly choir left a few presents behind
> . . . . . . . . . . . . . . .
> Bread is a fruit of the earth, yet touched by the blessings
>     of sunlight,

And from the thundering god issues the gladness of
  wine.
Therefore, too, these raise up our thought to the
  heavenly, those who
Once were here and at last shall return when their
  advent is due.
. . . . . . . . . . . . . . . . . . . . .
Meanwhile, bearing the torch, yet does the Son of the
  Highest,
Yet does the Syrian descend here to the shadows
  below.²³

The bread and the wine left by the gods are the body and the blood of Christ. Can the hidden truth of Christianity be the *en kai pan*, the vision of which had departed with the gods of Greece, and in token of which they have left the bread and the wine? Is *en kai pan* the truth of the Christian revelation? This, then, was Hölderlin's religion. As we shall see it was also Hegel's, and as we shall also see, the fundamental question which Hegel asked in politics was whether it was possible for Christianity as it has historically developed to be the kind of religion which reconciles, and which heals the rift in man. As he asked in an early writing, Is Judaea the Teuton Fatherland?

### Notes

1 Lessing, *The Education of the Human Race*, para 91.
2 Ibid., para 92.
3 Ibid., para 94.
4 Ibid., para 98.
5 Ibid., para 100.
6 'One and All'. Lessing carved *En kai pan* on the door of a friend's summerhouse on a visit shortly afterwards together with Jacobi.
7 Lessing, *On the reality of things outside God* (1763). Published posthumously (in 1795). Quelle que soit la manière dont je m'expliquerais la réalité des choses en dehors de Dieu, je dois avouer que je ne puis m'en faire une idée.

8 The abode of the dead.
9 Friedrich Hölderlin, *His Poems*, trans. Michael Hamburger with a critical study of the poet (London, The Harvill Press, 1952), p. 54.
10 Friedrich Hölderlin, *Hyperion*, trans. Willard R. Trask (New York and Toronto, The New American Library, 1965), pp. 163–5.
11 Ibid., p. 94.
12 These extracts appeared without commentary in the manuscript.
13 Hölderlin, *Hyperion*, p. 23.
14 Ibid., p. 93.
15 Ibid., p. 101.
16 Ibid., p. 152.
17 Ibid., p. 159.
18 Ibid., p. 158.
19 Ibid., p. 170 (Conclusion).
20 Ibid., p. 76.
21 Ibid., p. 45.
22 Ibid., p. 108.
23 Hölderlin, *His Poems*, pp. 145–55.

# 6

# HEGEL'S THOUGHT

I want now to begin to consider the character of Hegel's political thought. Acquaintance with this thought sooner or later leads to the conclusion that it exhibits remarkable continuity. *The Philosophy of Right*, which Hegel published in 1821, may be taken as his systematic and mature account of politics and its place in human experience. It contains themes and raises issues which are already present in the Iena lectures of 1803–4 and 1805–6 and in the unpublished writings of the Frankfurt period 1797–1800, and some are even to be found in the unpublished writings of the preceding Berne period. But if we can say that Hegel as a thinker attained maturity fairly early, that by the age of 30 he had formulated those ideas which were to make him the most original modern philosopher and one of the most fertile in influence over the intellectual life of Europe, yet we have also to say that these original ideas of his have their matrix or origin in other ideas of his which he outgrew and abandoned.

My business here is to study the political thought of Hegel and Marx, and this, as I have said in my first lecture, means in the first place to find out which Hegelian ideas were mediated to Marx, and in what manner they were mediated. But in the second place the enterprise also involves examining how, unbeknown to himself, the young Marx (in reacting as he thought against Hegelianism) echoed certain ideas of the young Hegel – ideas which the older Hegel abandoned as inadequate, but which (by contrast) constitute the foundation of Marx's mature thought.

It is only now, in this sixth lecture, that I am beginning to approach Hegel's own thought. What I have done so far is to examine some of the intellectual context which surrounds – and serves to situate and account for – Hegel's thought. This manner of proceeding may be likened to modern building operations in which for months on end you see building workers engaged on a laborious task which seems to be no more than digging holes in the ground, and which proves in the end to be the indispensable groundwork for the structure which begins soon thereafter to take shape quickly before our eyes. Or, in justification of this proceeding, I may once again remind you of Hegel's programmatic statement that philosophy is a circle – a statement the corollary of which is that the straight line is an impediment to the understanding. Or as Eliot put it in the same poem from which I quoted in the last lecture,

> We shall not cease from exploration
> And the end of all our exploring
> Will be to arrive where we started
> And know the place for the first time.

Or again, to make use of an argument which, as we saw, Lessing used in *The Education of the Human Race*, we may say that the themes which we saw occurring in Schiller, Lessing and Hölderlin constitute, if we but knew how to appreciate their full meaning and implications, a prefiguration, a fresh dawning of the main themes which the philosopher was to develop, enrich and deepen.

# Hegel's Thought

I ended the last lecture by arguing that the religion of *en kai pan*, of the one-and-all, all ones enfolding themselves in the all, and the all unfolding itself in many ones, was Hölderlin's religion. Of this we have many indications.

In August 1796, while still with his Berne employers, Hegel wrote a long poem, 100 lines long, dedicated in gratitude to his friend Hölderlin who had succeeded in obtaining for him a tutor's post in Frankfurt. The poem is entitled *Eleusis*,[1] in obvious reference to the Eleusinian mysteries by which the ancient Greeks celebrated the cult of Demeter and her daughter Persephone, who was taken by Hades the death-god to the underworld, and whom Zeus arranges to return to her grief-stricken mother. These mysteries have clearly to do with death and rebirth, and scholars say that in time the mysteries came to have something to do with the hope of human immortality – that immortality which the religion of *en kai pan* promises to its devotees, who cannot vanish into nothingness because they are for ever part of the ever-enduring, ever-embracing all.

Hegel's poem contains many themes, not all of which are relevant to our present purpose. Hegel begins by expressing his longing to meet his friend, and imagines the circumstances of their forthcoming meeting, and what joy they will feel to discover how they have both been faithful to their vow:

> To live for nothing but the free truth, and never, never to make peace
> With dogma which governs opinions and sentiments.[2]

But the author, who is contemplating by moonlight Lake Bienne, by which he is sitting, soon forgets himself in the contemplation of nature:

> What I called 'I' vanishes, I abandon myself to the incommensurable

> I am in it, I am the all,
> I am nothing but it.³

When his spirit comes back, it is like a stranger, having lost itself in the contemplation of Eternity. Then comes a long invocation to Persephone, a hope that the doors of her sanctuary would open to the faithful.

> Drunk with exaltation, I would now experience
> The shudder [which heralds] your coming.
> I would understand your revelations
> And would interpret the high
> Significance of your images; I would
> learn the hymns which are sung during the repast of the
>   Gods
> The noble decrees of their council.
> Alas, your dwellings O Goddess, have become silent
> Deserting the consecrated altars
> The company of the Gods has gone back to Olympus
> Because the genius of innocence which has attracted
>   them here
> Has forsaken the tomb of a profaned humanity.⁴

The secret of Persephone and her mysteries is now kept only by a few who keep it in the sanctuary of their heart. It is in their actions that the goddess continues to live.

> And tonight also, O holy Goddess, you have appeared to
>   me
> And it is you also who reveal to me the life of your
>   children
> You whom I feel to be the soul of their actions!
> You are the profound spirit, the faith which keeps faith,
> Which, being a Divinity, even when everything falls
>   down, remain steady.⁵

Clearly the goddess whom Hegel so fervently invokes is, among other things, the All in which individual men find their (everlasting) being. This pantheism is clearly something with which Hegel assumes his friend to be familiar – and, as we have seen from *Hyperion* and his other writings, this was in fact the case. But neither Hegel's poem, nor Hölderlin's writings do more than express this religion by means of image, allusion and metaphor. Can we find something in Hegel which would describe the beliefs of such a religion in a set of propositions rather than in imaginative language?

As it happens we can. We may perhaps begin by a text which Hegel did not write, but which rather he copied into his notebooks. This is a passage from Mosheim's *Ecclesiastical History* (which was published in 1764) relating to the medieval sect known as the Brethren of the Free Spirit, whose teachings the Church condemned as heretical.[6] These men, Mosheim wrote, prided themselves on being delivered from the yoke of the Law and having obtained Liberty of the Spirit. Their theology was founded on philosophical actions very similar 'to the impious error of those who are known as pantheists'.

> They taught that all things emanated from God, and were destined to return to him; spirits endowed with reason were parts of the Supreme Power itself, and *the universal totality of things is God*. By elevating his soul and putting it at a distance from the world of the senses, man is able to unite himself in an ineffable mode with him who has engendered and caused the universe, to the point of being identified with him. Those who, through a long contemplation, have plunged into the abyss of Divinity, obtain the supreme liberty and find themselves freed not only from all passions, but also even from the natural instincts. From all these and similar considerations they concluded that a man who in this way is raised up to God, and as though absorbed by the divine nature is himself God, and similar to Christ the son of God.

To this description of the tenets of the Brethren of the Free Spirit, Mosheim added two extracts from their writings which Hegel also copied. The first is from 'their more secret books' and it goes like this:

> The good man is God's only son whom the Father has begotten from all eternity.... There is something in the souls which has not been created, and which cannot be created: this is their rational character. God is neither good nor better, nor the best possible; I am therefore unjust if I call him good, as if, knowing (whether I myself or Him) that a thing is white, I called it black. Even now, the Father begets his Son, and the same Son. Because what God produces is one.... What Holy Writ declares of Christ can be said with equal truth of every one of the divine men. What is proper to divine nature is proper to every divine man.

The second extract comes from a text of 1317 which was condemned at the time by a bishop of Strasbourg as heretical:

> Formally, God is all that exists. Every perfect man is Christ by nature. The perfect man is free in respect of everything and is not required to observe the precepts which are ordained by God. In the Gospel there are many poetical things which are not true, and men should believe in the concepts which are born from their soul united with God, more than in the Gospel.

The interest of these quotations from Mosheim is that they indicate for us the kind of ideas which were preoccupying Hegel during his Berne and Frankfurt period. We are not of course to understand from these quotations that Hegel subscribed to the doctrines of the Brethren of the Free Spirit as they are described in Mosheim, but rather that he found in them a way of reworking the arid and objectionable theology of the Stift, and transforming it into something philosophically tenable and humanly satisfying. And this is what we see him doing on his own account in the writing known as

*The Spirit of Christianity and its Fate*, which dates from the Frankfurt period, the period during which, as we remember, Hegel emerges as an original thinker. One of the sections of this writing is entitled *The Religious Teaching of Jesus*, and it is here that we see Hegel attempting by patient and skilful exegesis to show that the essence of Jesus' teaching can be nothing but the unity of man and God, a unity which is possible because it is only like which unites with like; in other words that God and man share the same substance. We may say that here Hegel is providing the philosophical counterpart or justification of the idea suggested to us by Hölderlin's poem *Bread and Wine*, that Christianity is in truth only another form of Greek religion, a religion in which the gods were not withdrawn in a sphere higher than that of men, but in fact dwelt among men, and had familiar intercourse with them – in a world where gods and men were equally at home, and this because the world embraced them both in a common fellowship (*en kai pan*) in which there was no heaven above the earth, no lordship and bondage, no master and servant, no separation, no estrangement, no division.

Hegel begins by saying that Jesus brought a new teaching fundamentally different from that of Judaism: 'To the Jewish idea of God as their Lord and Governor, Jesus opposes a relationship of God to men similar to that of a father to his children.'[7]

And Hegel proceeds to explore the full implications of fathership and sonship in the relations between God and man. He points out that 'the most commonly cited and the most striking expression of Jesus' relation to God is his calling himself the "son of God".'[8] Now, 'the relation of a son to his father is not a conceptual unity (as, for instance, unity or harmony of disposition, similarity of principles etc.), a unity which is only a unity in thought and is abstracted from life. On the contrary, it is a living relation of living beings, a likeness of life.' We may note here Hegel's emphasis on life as opposed to concept. Life, if we may so put it, is living while the concept is a dead abstraction. The ideas of life, of love as the only proper relation of living beings, of spirit as that which exclusively grasps another spirit, this idea and this vocabulary loom very large in Hegel's thinking in this period, and we may even say that life – as self-consciousness, not as a biological manifestation – love and spirit are interchangeable ideas for him, though it is the word 'spirit' or 'mind' – as the word *Geist* has unavoidably to be translated – which will loom largest later on, beginning let us say with the *Phenomenology of Mind* (*Phänomenologie des Geistes*) of 1807.

'Father and son', to continue Hegel's argument, 'are simply modifications of the same life, not opposite essences. . . . Thus the son of God is the same essence as the father.' To explain what he means by this Hegel instances the expression in use among the Arabs, 'a son of the stem of Koresh'. This expression is used to denote the individual, the member of the clan, and in this expression 'there is the implication that this individual is not simply part of the whole; the whole does not lie outside him; he himself is just the whole which the entire clan is'. Thus, when waging war such a people does not have regard to individuals. A defeated clan is all put to the sword. This is in contrast to modern Europe 'where each individual does not carry the whole state in himself, but where the bond is only the conceptual one of the same rights for all'. Here, 'war is waged not against the individual, but against the whole which lies outside him. *As with any genuinely free people*, so among the Arabs, *the individual is a part and at the same time the whole.*' This is life, and 'What is a contradiction in the realm of the dead is not one in the realm of life.'

> A tree which has three branches makes up with them one tree; but every 'son' of the tree, every branch (and also its other 'children', leaves and blossoms) is itself a tree. The fibres bringing sap to the branch from the stem are of the same nature as the roots. If a [cutting from certain types of] tree is set on the ground upside down it will put forth leaves out of the roots in the air, and the boughs will root themselves in the ground. And it is just as true to say that there is only one tree here as to say that there are three.⁹

A passage such as this will, incidentally, be of great help to us when we seek to understand an idea of Hegel's as rich and complex as that of the 'concrete universal' which looms so large in his writings about man and society.¹⁰

Jesus the son of God is thus one with God – of the same essence as God.

> When Jesus said: 'The father is in me and I in the father; who has seen me has seen the father; who knows the father knows that what I say is true; I and the father are one,' the Jews accused him of blasphemy because though born a man he made himself God.¹¹

But Hegel says Jewish objections were of no substance:

> The hill and the eye which sees it are object and subject, but between man and God, between spirit and spirit, there is no such cleft of objectivity and subjectivity; *one is to the other an other only in that one recognizes the other*; both are one.

There are three steps by which Hegel establishes that God equals Jesus equals Man.

1. The essence of Jesus, i.e. his relationship to God as son to father, can be truly grasped only by faith.

2. This faith is characterized by its object [*Gegenstand*], the divine. Faith in a mundane reality is an acquaintance with some kind of object [*Objekt*], of

something restricted. And just as an object [*Objekt*] is other than God, so this acquaintance is different from faith in the divine.

3. 'God is spirit, and they that worship him must worship him in spirit and in truth.' How could anything but a spirit know a spirit? . . . Faith in the divine is only possible if in the believer himself there is a divine element which rediscovers itself. . . . In every man there is light and life; he is the property of the light. He is not illuminated by a light in the way in which a dark body is when it borrows a brightness not its own; on the contrary, his own inflammability takes fire and he burns with a flame that is his own. . . . Hence faith in the divine grows out of the divinity of the believer's own nature; *only a modification of the Godhead can know the Godhead.*[12]

The faith which Jesus' friends have in him and therefore in God is the first stage in their relationship. Hegel quotes John 12: 36,[13] 'Until ye have light, believe in the light, that ye may be children of light.' There is a difference between those who only have faith in the light and those who are children of light. Jesus wanted to see his followers actually children of the light. John's account of his final discourse indicates what he aspired to for them: 'They in him and he in them; they together one; he the vine, they the branches; in the parts of the same nature, a life like the life in the whole.' 'So long as Jesus lived among his friends, they remained believers only, *for they were not self-dependent*. Jesus was their teacher and master, an individual center on which they depended. They had not yet attained an independent life of their own.' But after his death 'even this objectivity, this partition between them and God, fell away, and the spirit of God could then animate their whole being'. In such an existence, 'the opposition of seer and seen, i.e. of subject and object, disappears in the seeing itself. Their difference is only a possibility of separation. A man wholly immersed in seeing the sun would be only a feeling of light, would be light-feeling become an entity. A man who lived entirely in beholding another would be this other entirely, would be merely possessed of the possibility of becoming different from him.'[14] This relationship of Jesus' followers is 'beautiful' and a 'harmony', an 'association with the divine'. Referring to Matthew 10: 41 (He that receiveth a prophet in the name of a prophet shall receive a prophet's reward), Hegel provides his own interpretation: 'Where two or three are united in my spirit, in that respect in which being and eternal life shall fall to my lot, in which I *am*, then I am in the midst of them, and so is my spirit.' The conclusion that Hegel draws from this chain of reasoning is that Jesus declared himself 'against personality, against the view that his essence possessed an individuality opposed to that of those who had attained the culmination of friendship with him (*against the thought of a personal God*)'.

When a community is bound by these ties of friendship, this is 'the culmination of faith, the return to the Godhead whence man is born'. This 'closes the circle of man's development. Everything lives in the Godhead, every living thing is its child.'[15] The circle 'begins with faith in gods outside itself [the child], with fear, until through its actions it has [isolated and] separated itself more and more; but then it returns through associations to the original unity which is now developed, self-produced, and sensed as unity. The child now knows God, i.e., the spirit of God is present in the child, issues from its restrictions, annuls the modification, and restores the whole. God, the Son, the Holy Spirit.' Or *en kai pan*.

As we shall see, Hegel believed that the reconciliation, the union, the concord which Jesus wanted to bring to men came to nought, and was *fated* to come to nought. But to this point we shall return. What I would like to stress is how much this vision of men working to attain a living communion with their fellow men and thus becoming divine and immortal remained Hegel's ruling vision and the thread by which he was guided in trying to form for himself a coherent account of human history, itself the product of the human mind. Thus he tells us in the preface of the *Phenomenology* that the element and content of philosophy is 'the real, what is self-establishing, has life within itself, existence in its very notion. It is the process that creates its own moments in its course, and goes through them all; and the whole of this movement constitutes its positive content and its truth. . . . Appearance is the process of arising into being and passing away again, a process that itself does not arise and does not pass away, but is *per se*, and constitutes reality and the life-movement of truth. The truth', as he says in a famous image, 'is thus the bacchanalian revel, where not a member is sober; and because every member no sooner becomes detached that it *eo ipso* collapses straightway, the revel is just as much a state of transparent unbroken calm.'[16] Or again in the last paragraph of the introduction: 'The experience which consciousness has concerning itself can, by its essential principle, embrace nothing less than the entire system of consciousness, the whole realm of the truth of mind. . . . In pressing forward to its true form of existence, consciousness will come to a point at which it lays aside its semblance of being hampered with what is foreign to it . . . it will reach a position where appearance becomes identified with essence. . . . And, finally, when it grasps this its own essence, it will connote the nature of absolute knowledge itself.'[17]

It is by means of philosophy, and not of religion, Hegel came to believe, that mind, spirit, *Geist*, attains full self-awareness and absolute knowledge, which is self-knowledge. But *Geist* is not any individual's spirit. *Geist* is rather the spirit, the life, which flows through all living men, which all living men share. The absolute self-knowledge of *Geist* cannot therefore be an individual's solitary self-awareness – it is rather a bacchanalian revel, and the revellers are the totality of mankind. In the second place this self-awareness and self-control is not (as in Schiller) a matter of contemplation but rather of doing. Self-knowledge, absolute knowledge, is practical as well as theoretical, acting as well as thinking. Doing, indeed we may even say the most important kind of doing, consists in those steps which men take in order to make themselves at home in the world. This way of putting it is as good as any in describing what for Hegel constitutes the end of philosophy as well as of action politics. What can be said about men's attempts to accomplish this?

## Notes

1 See G. E. Mueller, *Hegel: The Man, His Vision and Work* (New York, Pageant Press Inc., 1968) for an English translation. Another English version of the poem appears in *Hegel: The Letters*, trans. C. Butler and C. Seiler (Bloomington, Indiana University Press, 1984), pp. 46–7. Neither translation, however, is the one used by E. K. We have so far failed to trace the source he used – Eds.
2 verses 20–1.
3 verses 31–4.
4 verses 45–55.
5 verses 100–105.
6 P. Asveld, *La pensée religieuse du jeune Hegel* (Louvain, Publ. Univ., 1953), pp. 128–30.
7 Knox and Kroner, p. 253.
8 Ibid., pp. 259–60.
9 Ibid., p. 261.

10 Schiller's *Aesthetic Education*. The dancer and the dance. The living leaf and the dead leaf (Knox and Kroner, p. 265).
11 Knox and Kroner, p. 265.
12 Ibid., p. 266.
13 Ibid., p. 268.
14 Ibid., p. 270.
15 Ibid., p. 273.
16 G. W. F. Hegel, *The Phenomenology of Mind*, trans. J. B. Baillie (London, George Allen & Unwin, 1971), p. 105.
17 Ibid., pp. 144–5.

# 7

# HEGEL AND RELIGION

During his last year at the Tübinger Stift (1792–3), or perhaps in the long vacation before he went to take up his post of tutor in Berne, Hegel wrote a long essay which his editor, Nohl, entitled 'Folk-Religion and Christianity'. It is not important for us here to consider how appropriate this title is, or whether it does justice to Hegel's concerns in this essay. What is quite clear is that the essay is concerned with religion. It begins with these words: 'Religion is one of the most important concerns of our life.' In order to discuss how this most important concern is best taken care of, Hegel begins by making a distinction between objective and subjective religion:

> Objective religion is *fides quae creditur* [the faith that is held], the understanding and the memory are the powers that are operative in it, they examine evidences, think it through and preserve it . . . objective religion suffers itself to be arranged in one's mind, organized into a system, set forth in a book, and expounded to others in a discourse; *subjective religion expresses itself only in feelings and actions* – if I say of a man that he has religion, this does not mean that he has much knowledge about it, but rather that he feels in his heart the seeds, the miracles, the nearness of the Deity, *his heart knows and sees God in its own nature, in the destinies of men.* . . . Subjective religion is alive, it is effective in the

inwardness of our being, and active in our outward behaviour. Subjective religion is fully individuated, objective religion is abstraction: the former is the living book of nature, plants, insects, birds and beasts, as they live with one another and upon one another... the latter is the cabinet of the naturalist wherein the insects have been killed, the plants dried, the animals stuffed or pickled, – and the things that nature divided are put side by side – all organized for one single end where nature had interlaced an infinite variety of ends in a friendly bond.[1]

Objective religion, then, is dead. Subjective religion is alive. And Hegel's purpose, as he tells us, is to discover how objective religion can be made 'wholly subjective',[2] how it can 'enter into the web of human feelings, become associated with human impulses to action, and prove living and active in them'. So far as objective religion goes, the understanding, which for Hegel is to be distinguished from reason (a distinction he will work out later), will serve to sift out what is rational from what is superstitious, what is incoherent, unclear, paradoxical, self-contradictory. The understanding, he says, 'has brought forth noble fruits, Lessing's *Nathan*, and it deserves the eulogies which are continually offered in its name': 'But it is never through understanding that the principles are rendered practical.' The understanding and enlightenment can help us to avoid superstitions and a fetish faith, and to avoid such is no doubt a necessity in a religion; the doctrines of any religion 'must be grounded on universal Reason'; but if it is to be a subjective religion, 'Fancy, heart, and sensibility must not thereby go empty away.'[3] But that a religion should be subjective through and through is not enough.

These conditions by themselves lay down what is necessary for a *private* religion to be truly religion. But religion has to be more than private – it has to be *public*, it has to be the religion of a people – a *Volksreligion* – to be embodied in the soul of a people.[4] Thirdly, therefore, 'it must be so constituted that all the needs of life – the public affairs of the state are tied in with it.' What religion fulfils these specifications? Hegel is absolutely clear that Christianity does not fill them. In Christianity there is a wall between 'life and doctrine'. It is occupied with 'idle word-games',[5] demands 'a level of piety . . . that is hypocritical because it is too high'; it is in conflict with the natural needs of men, it is 'too gloomy on its outward side to dare give any pledge that men would surrender the joys of life in response to its demands'.

To be able to fulfil its functions, 'religion must abide in amity with all the emotions of life – not want to force its way in – but be everywhere welcome.' It must not be 'like a harsh school-governess',[6] it must generate and nourish noble dispositions, and go hand in hand with freedom. For Hegel such a religion existed once, long before Christianity; it existed in Athens.

The spirit of the people, Hegel tells us, is its history, its religion, the level of its political freedom. These things are woven together in a single bond.

> The father of this Genius [or spirit] is Time on which he remains dependent in a way all his life . . . – his mother the *politeia*, the Constitution – his mid-wife, his wet-nurse, Religion – who took the fine arts into her service to aid in his education – and the music of physical and spiritual motion – . . . that is drawn down to the earth and held fast by a light bond which resists through a magic spell all attempts to break it for it is completely intertwined in his essence. This bond, whose main foundations are our needs, is woven together from the manifold threads of nature.[7]

This genius is 'a son of fortune and freedom, a pupil of beautiful fancy. The brazen bond of his needs fetters him . . . to Mother Earth, but he worked over it, refined it, beautifying it with feeling and fancy, twining it with roses by the aid of the Graces, so that he could delight in these fetters as his own work, as a part of himself.'[8] This spirit, this *Volkgeist*, received from his father Time 'faith in his fortune and pride in his deeds'. 'His indulgent mother', woman [the Constitution], was 'no scolding, harsh woman' and 'left her son to the education of nature, and did not swaddle his delicate limbs in tight bands.'

> In harmony with her the wet-nurse [Religion] could not rear the child of nature, or seek to bring him up to adolescence with [such methods as] the fear of the rod or of a ghost in the dark, nor [did she feed him] on the sour-sweet sugar-bread of mysticism that weakens the stomach – nor did she keep him in the leading reins of words, which would have made him forever a minor – but she gave him the cleaner more wholesome milk of pure feelings to drink. . . . As the nurse in a Greek household remained in the family circle and was a friend to her charge all his life, so was she [Religion] ever his [the Greek spirit's] friend, and he offered her his thanks and his love with unspoiled spontaneity, he shared his joys and his games with her as a friendly comrade and was not kept from his joys by her – but she kept her dignity inviolate, and his own conscience punished every slight toil – she kept her authority always, for it was founded on love and gratitude, on the noblest emotions of her charge – she flattered his finery – heeded the humours of his fancy – but she taught him to follow the path of unalterable destiny without grumbling.[9]

The Greek genius, then, is the summit of the human spirit. And it is not only this passage which is indicative of Hegel's passion for Greece. To look at other passages is only to confirm the impression which this passage produces. Consider the epithets with which Hegel was to describe Greece, Greek religion and the polis: 'beautiful, noble, sublime, great, delicate, soft, tender, human, open, subtle'. Joy, freedom, goodness, plenitude, life, power, enjoyment, characterize this genius and its products. But, alas, this spirit is now departed, and the 23-year-old Hegel pens an elegy for him as eloquent as any written by his friend Hölderlin:

> We know this Genius only by hearsay, only a few traits of his character are we permitted to gaze on in love and wonder in surviving copies of his form, [traces] which merely awaken a *sorrowful yearning* for the original – He is the beautiful youth, whom we love even in his thoughtless moments, along with the whole company of the Graces, and with them the balsam breath of nature, the soul, which is inspired by them, he sucked from every flower, he is flown from the earth.[10]

Whatever the regrets, and however great the yearning, this genius, this spirit is no more, is dead and gone, and to revive it *as it was* is utterly impossible. What has taken its place is something for which Hegel has no affection, has even revulsion. For the essay concludes with a passage which, though it ends in mid-sentence, leaves us in no doubt about Hegel's strong feelings:

> A different Genius of the nations has the West hatched – his form is aged – beautiful he never was – but some slight touches of manliness remain still faintly traceable in him – his father is bowed [with age] – he [the Western Genius?] dares not stand up straight either to look around gaily at the world nor from a sense of his own dignity – he is short-sighted and can see only little things one at a time – without courage, without confidence in his own strength, he hazards no bold throw, iron fetters raw and [here the manuscript ends][11]

Why is this Western genius so ugly and old? Again Hegel leaves us in no doubt: its horrible characteristics derive from Christianity. In this essay and elsewhere he expresses himself in a way such as to leave us in no doubt of his revulsion and antipathy for traditional orthodox Christianity. In this very essay, there is a passage which immediately precedes the dithyramb about the genius of Greece which I have just quoted. It goes like this:

> Our religion aims to educate men to be citizens of Heaven whose gaze is ever directed thither so that human feelings become alien to them. At our greatest public festival, one draws near to enjoy the heavenly gifts, in a garb of mourning and with lowered gaze – at the festival – which ought to be the feast of universal brotherhood – many a man is afraid he will catch from the common cup the venereal infection of the one who drank before him, so that his mind is not attentive, not occupied with holy feelings, and during the function itself he must reach into his pocket and by his offering on the plate – unlike the Greeks with the friendly gifts of nature – crowned with flowers and arrayed in joyful colours – radiating gaiety from open faces that invited all to love and friendship – [thus] they approached the altars of their benevolent gods.

The question then arises – how did all this happen? How did a religion like Christianity – so inimical to human happiness, so ugly, so crude, so prone to servility and superstition – supplant the Greek religion with all its beauty and delicacy, a religion so favourable to happiness and freedom? In Berne, where Hegel was from 1793 to 1797, he continued his religious studies, the fruits of which were a Life of Jesus and the writing entitled *The Positivity of the Christian Religion*. These writings are devoted to exploring the question as to the exact character of Jesus' teaching, the relation of this teaching to what the Church later taught, and the reasons for the spread of this teaching. The supplanting of paganism by Christianity was, Hegel tells us, a 'remarkable' revolution. 'The supersession of a native and immemorial religion by a foreign one is a revolution which occurs in the spiritual realm itself' and its causes must be found in the spirit of the times. Such a great revolution, again, must have been preceded 'by a still and secret revolution' in the spirit of the age. Hegel is impressed by this still and secret revolution by which Christianity supplanted a religion which had been established in states for centuries and intimately connected with their constitutions. 'What', he asks, 'can have caused the cessation of a belief in gods to whom cities and empires ascribed their origin, to whom the people made daily offerings . . . under whose banners alone the armies had conquered, who had been thanked for victories . . . and whose worship and festivals were but occasions for universal joy?'[12]

The pagan religion is a religion for free men. As free men the Greeks and Romans 'obeyed laws laid down by themselves, obeyed men whom they had themselves appointed to office, waged wars on which they had themselves decided, gave their property, exhausted their passions, and sacrificed their lives by thousands for an end which was their own'. For a free man of this kind 'the idea of his country or of his state was the invisible and higher reality for which he strove . . . it was the final end of *his* world . . . an end which he manifested in the realities of his daily life or which he himself co-operated in manifesting and maintaining.' A man's individuality did not count here. 'It was only this idea's maintenance, life, and persistence that he asked for. . . . It could never or hardly ever have struck him to ask or beg for persistence or eternal life for his own individuality.'[13] Increase of wealth, luxury, fortunate wars created in Athens and Rome an aristocracy of wealth and much glory to whom the masses gradually ceded pre-eminence

– and republican regions fell into decay. A professional bureaucracy arises, together with hierarchy and private interests. 'Usefulness to the state, was the great end which the state set before its subjects, and the end they set before themselves in their political life was gain, self-maintenance and perhaps vanity.'[14] 'Activity was no longer for the sake of an ideal.' Every one worked for himself and freedom to obey self-given laws and to share in the affairs of the republic disappeared.

> All political freedom vanished also; the citizen's right gave him only a right to the security of that property which now filled his entire world. Death, the phenomenon which demolished the whole structure of his purposes and the activity of his entire life, must have become something terrifying, since nothing survived him. But the republican's whole soul was in the republic; the republic survived him, and there hovered before his mind the thought of its immortality.[15]

It is at that point, when division in the state, in society and in the soul was rife, that Christianity appeared on the stage. Men gave up their moral autonomy to a God in heaven, as they had given up their political autonomy to their emperor. God became 'a being foreign to us' dwelling in heaven with whom men have nothing in common.[16]

> Thus the despotism of the Roman emperors had chased the human spirit from the earth and spread a misery which compelled men to seek and expect happiness in heaven; robbed of freedom, their spirit, their eternal and absolute element was freed to take flight to the deity. [The doctrine of] God's objectivity is a counterpart to the corruption and slavery of man.... The spirit of the age was revealed in its objective conception of God when he was no longer regarded as like ourselves, though infinitely greater, but was put into another world in

whose confines we had no part, to which we contributed nothing by our activity, but into which, at best, we could beg or conjure our way. . . . Its most dreadful revelation was when on this God's behalf men fought, murdered, defamed, burned at the stake, stole, lied and betrayed. In a period like this, God must have ceased altogether to be something subjective and have entirely become an object.[17]

But this Christianity, this objective, utterly objective, religion, a religion for men under despotism, for slaves, what relation does it have to what Jesus taught? *The Spirit of Christianity and its Fate*, written during the Frankfurt period (1797–9), offered a complicated, subtle and unusual interpretation of Jesus' teaching. Jesus, on this interpretation, taught the unity of man and God, in a communion of love, a communion of love in which Jesus, God his father, and his friends and followers partook in one another's nature. In the Berne period Hegel had had another view of Jesus' teaching. In this view Jesus was a kind of Kantian, who tried to bring men to a knowledge of their own moral autonomy. 'He undertook to raise religion and virtue to morality and to restore to morality the freedom which is its essence. 'His 'simple doctrine' required 'renunciation, sacrifice, and a struggle against inclinations'.[18] Jesus urged 'a free virtue springing from man's own being'. But this teaching of Jesus' which tried to instil freedom and autonomy of the will ended by becoming a *positive* religion, 'i.e.,' says Hegel, 'a religion which is grounded in authority and puts man's worth not at all, or at least not wholly in morals'.[19] How did this happen? Hegel says that in order to gain the Jews to his message, Jesus had to claim that it constituted the will of God, he had to claim to be the Messiah, and to perform miracles. His disciples accepted his message not because it was rational – they were too limited to understand that – but on the authority of their teacher. There is a great contrast here with Socrates and his friends who 'loved Socrates because of his virtue and philosophy, not virtue and his philosophy because of him'.[20] All these things made Christianity into a positive religion fit for *private* men who had lost all political freedom and wholeness of spirit under the despotism of the Roman empire. On this view Jesus therefore failed, and his failure stemmed from the contradiction between the character of his teaching and the conditions under which it had to take place.

In *The Spirit of Christianity and its Fate* Hegel still believes that Christianity became a positive religion fairly soon after Jesus' death, but his reasons are different here, deeper, more complex, and with widespread implications. The message of Jesus was love. But the Jews, his people, did not listen to this message, except for a small group whom he sent to preach the Kingdom of God. But their preaching is received with indifference and then with hatred.[21] When the disciples return empty-handed, he renounces his people and has the feeling that God reveals himself only to the simple-minded. He restricts himself to working on individuals. He flees the world and cuts himself off from his nation. His sole relationship with the state was to remain under its jurisdiction.

> The Kingdom of God is not of this world, only it makes a great difference for that Kingdom whether this world is actually present in opposition to it, or whether its opposition does not exist but is only a possibility. The former was in fact the case, and it was with full knowledge of this that Jesus suffered at the hands of the state. Hence with this [passive] relation to the state one great element in a living union is cut away; for the members of the Kingdom of God one important bond of association is snapped; they have lost one part of freedom . . . ; they have lost a number of active

relationships and living ties. The citizens of the Kingdom of God become set over against a hostile state, *become private persons excluding themselves from it.*

'The State was there and neither Jesus nor his following could annul it' and therefore 'the fate of Jesus and his following remains a loss of freedom, a restriction of life, passivity under the domination of an alien might.'[22]

Thus Jesus' gospel of love is not enough. It will not heal the rift in the body politic, or the body social, and not the rift in the soul. And that union between God and man which Jesus preached and which was the hallmark of the Greek religion is still unattainable. Passivity is not a way out. It is *fated* to lead to rift and division.

But there are yet other things to be said about the unsatisfactory character of this gospel of love. Consider *the fate* of the friends of Jesus after his death. They established brotherhoods, some of which abolished property rights against one another. 'They conversed about their departed friend and master, prayed together, strengthened one another in faith and courage. Their enemies accused some of their societies of even having wives in common, *an accusation which they lacked purity and courage enough to deserve, or of which they had no need to feel shame.*'[23] They proselytized, they prayed, they ate together. But beyond this there is an immense field of activity for man. But this community as such cannot engage in this activity. It cannot go beyond love itself. Every other tie is alien to such a community 'whether the purpose of such a tie be the achievement of some end or the development of another side of life or a common activity. Equally alien is every spirit of co-operation for something other than the dissemination of the faith, every spirit which reveals and enjoys itself in play in other modes and restricted forms of life.' Such activity would have led to the renunciation of love, and its destruction because in the pursuit of such activities 'the members would have put themselves in jeopardy of clashing against one another's individuality'. Love might therefore have been changed into hatred 'and a severance from God would have followed. This danger is warded off by an inactive and undeveloped love, i.e., by a love which, though love is the highest life, remains unliving.'

> Hence the contra-natural expansion of love's scope becomes entangled in a contradiction, in a false effort, which was bound to become the father of the most appalling fanaticism, whether of an active or a passive life. This restriction of love to itself, its flight from all determinate modes of living *even if its spirit breathed in them, or even if they sprang from its spirit, this removal of itself from all fate, is just its greater fate*; and here is the point where Jesus is linked with fate.[24]

Fate is that over which we have no control, but it may be the unintended outcome of our actions.

The religion which Jesus brought, the religion of love, is not enough. It will not answer for the reasons I have set out and for another reason. Christianity has not succeeded in effecting the union of subject and object which made the strength of Greek religion.[25] In an Apollo or a Venus we have an image in which seeing and feeling are unified. We see in the shape the immortal, and are permeated with the sense of love and eternal youth. But the bread and the wine, they are different. Bread has a mystical significance and is at the same time edible: 'after enjoying the supper, Christians today feel a reverent wonder, either without serenity or else with a melancholy serenity, because feeling's intensity was separate from the intellect and both were one-sided, because worship was incomplete, *since something divine was promised and it melted away in the mouth*.'[26]

Again, because this love was unliving, a mere taste in the mouth, for the group to keep together it needed to depend on a common founder set over against itself. In its spirit lay the consciousness of discipleship and of a lord and master. This is 'something positive, an object which has in it as much foreignness, as much dominion as there is dependence in the spirit of the group. In this community of dependence, the community of having a common founder... the group recognized its real bond and that assurance of unification which *could not be sensed in a love that was unliving.*'[27]

Greek religion and the polis are dead – and Christian love is no substitute. It is no substitute because it does not allow man to feel at home in the world. This was Jesus' aim, but he failed, failed because inherent in his attempt was failure. He was *fated* to fail. What then is to be done?

### Notes

1 H. S. Harris, *Hegel's Development: Towards the Sunlight 1770–1801* (Oxford, Clarendon Press, 1972), p. 484.
2 Ibid., p. 486.
3 Ibid., p. 499.
4 Ibid.
5 Ibid., p. 505.
6 Ibid.
7 Ibid., p. 506.
8 Ibid.
9 Ibid., p. 507.
10 Ibid.
11 Ibid.
12 Knox and Kroner, p. 152.
13 Ibid., p. 154.
14 Ibid., p. 156.
15 Ibid., p. 157.
16 Ibid., p. 160.
17 Ibid., p. 162–3.
18 Ibid., pp. 70–1.
19 Ibid., p. 71.

20 Ibid., p. 82.
21 Ibid., p. 283.
22 Ibid., p. 284.
23 Ibid., pp. 280–1.
24 Ibid., p. 281.
25 Ibid., pp. 252–3.
26 Appendix to *G. W. F. Hegel: L'esprit du christianisme et son destin*, with an introduction by J. Hyppolite, trans. J. Martin (Paris, Librarie Vrin). Religion, fonder une religion 138: Là où sujet et objet – où liberté et nature sont pensés comme liés de telle sorte que la nature soit liberté, que le sujet et l'objet ne soient pas séparables, là il y a du divin – un tel idéal est l'objet de toute religion.
27 Knox and Kroner, p. 295.

# 8

# RELIGION

Athens is dead and gone, and cannot be revived. The love preached by Jesus, Christian love, cannot make man feel at home in the world. It is an unliving, an inert love, which in the first place fates those who are bound by it to estrangement from their fellow men, and makes them incapable of developing any human activity or any enjoyment because these threaten the tie of love which is the supreme value of such a society. This religion of love, which in Jesus' teaching aimed to annul and transcend positivity, itself becomes positive – having to depend on a lord and master who is apart from and foreign to it – and this because the love binding it is unliving and inert.

Positivity, we may then say, is for Hegel the mark of failure in a religion. It is a mark of failure because the positive religion depends for its validity on an outside authority, on something alien, which human reason and human feelings cannot assimilate and penetrate. A positive religion is the sign of the absence of wholeness, of a rift both in the soul and in the body politic. Hegel developed this idea of positivity during his Berne period, in *The Positivity of the Christian Religion*. In this work Hegel argued that what Jesus really wanted was to bring men to an awareness of their own moral autonomy, to an understanding that the good is selflegislatory. 'The value of a virtuous disposition and the worthlessness of a hypocritical exactitude confined to merely external religious exercises were publicly taught by Jesus. . . . his simple doctrine . . . required renunciation, sacrifice and a struggle against inclination.' Jesus urged 'not a virtue grounded on authority (which is either meaningless or a direct contradiction in terms), but a free virtue springing from man's own being'.[1]

It is obvious that this view of Jesus' teaching is heavily indebted to Kant, and specifically to Kant's work, *Religion within the Bounds of Reason Alone*, 1793. There is little doubt that in *The Positivity of the Christian Religion* Hegel was continuing his warfare against traditional Christian theology, which in his eyes was a mere lifeless body, and which theologians like his teachers at the Tübinger Stift were in vain attempting to revive. Indeed we may even go further and say that Hegel's use of Kantian ideas here was a direct retort to one of his teachers at the Stift, G. C. Storr, who in a work published in 1794 attempted to make use of Kantian ideas in order to bolster the traditional orthodoxy.[2] Storr argued, among other things, that since theoretical reason (according to Kant) cannot know things-in-themselves, then it is powerless to declare the truth or falsity of doctrines such as that of divine revelation, resurrection, incarnation or the Trinity. Belief in these doctrines was a matter for the practical reason, and Storr claimed to establish that obedience to the moral law *required* belief in God and in Christ's divine authority and his miracles. Hegel clearly was concerned to show that on the contrary such beliefs were impediments to the true Christianity. But Hegel's target in this writing was more than just traditional theology. He was also intent on showing that positivity in religion leads to oppression in politics. In fact over half of *The Positivity of the Christian Church* is devoted to this subject. Churches, both Catholic and Protestant, have in fact become states with the power to exclude unbelievers and dissenters from the body politic, and to enforce belief and morality. Churches have authority to prescribe external actions and inner beliefs 'and Christians have thus reverted to the position of the Jews. The special characteristic of the Jewish religion – that bondage to law from which Christians so heartily congratulate themselves on being free – turns up once more in the Christian church.' The man who neglects the duties prescribed by the Church 'is burned at the stake in some places and is almost everywhere deprived of his political rights'. The churches go even further than the Jews: 'while the Jews thought they had satisfied God with their external ceremonies, it was impressed on the Christians that everything depended on the frame of mind in which two people performed the same action. . . . the main difference between Jews and Christians comes to this, that while in Judaism, only actions were commanded, the Christian church goes farther and commands feelings, a contradiction in terms. This difference is not of the kind which would achieve morality, the aim of moral philosophy and religion.'

In Berne therefore we see Hegel using Kant as a weapon with which to belabour the Christian churches and traditional Christian theology. But very shortly afterwards, we find Kant himself being accused of the same failings which his doctrine had been used to uncover within Christianity. If Christianity was in Berne denounced as a positive religion, we find that in Frankfurt Kant's philosophy is likewise denounced for its positivity. In *Religion within the Bounds of Reason Alone* Kant had declared that between the Shaman and the European prelate, between the Voguls and the Puritans, there was a great difference in manner, but none in principle; all alike they were obeying positive authorities, external commands, and not the law of their own reason. In *The Spirit of Christianity and its Fate* Hegel takes up this passage and aims it back straight at Kant. Hegel says of Jesus that 'against purely objective commands Jesus set something totally foreign to them, namely, the subjective in general.'³ But what Hegel now means by subjectivity is something much wider than the self-legislation or moral autonomy with which he was so much concerned in *The Positivity of the Christian Religion*. 'By this line of argument', that is, that a command as a concept is something subjective, the product of human power, thus losing its heteronomy and its positivity – 'By this line of argument, however, positivity is only partially removed; and between the Shaman of the Tungus, the European prelate who rules church and state, the Voguls and the Puritans, on the one hand, and the man who listens to his own command of duty, on the other, the difference is not that the former make themselves slaves, while the latter is free, but that the former have their lord outside themselves, while the latter carries his lord in himself, yet at the same time is his own slave.'⁴ The positivity of the Christian religion, then, has its counterpart in the positivity of the Kantian philosophy. And the heteronomy of external command is equalled by the heteronomy of inner command. For the impulses, the inclinations, pathological love, sensuous experience (all subsumed under the particular), the universal (that is, the law, whether an inner law or an external ordinance) is, Hegel argues, 'necessarily and always something alien and objective'. And the universal in exercising its sway 'excludes or dominates all other relations', and 'Woe to the human relations which are not unquestionably found in the concept of duty.' But such relations are still a part of what we understand by man, and this is why the Jesus of *The Spirit of*

*Christianity* has ceased to be the disciple of Immanuel Kant. 'To act in the spirit of the laws could not have meant for him "to act out of respect for duty and to contradict inclinations", for "both parts of the spirit" . . . just by being thus divergent would have been not in the spirit of the laws but against that spirit, one part [reason] because it was something exclusive and so self-restricted, the other [inclinations] because it was something repressed.' The spirit of Jesus is a spirit raised above morality. In the Sermon on the Mount Jesus directly attacks laws. The sermon is 'an attempt . . . to strip the laws of legality, of their legal form'. Jesus preaches love which is a modification of life,[5] that is life expressing itself in a specific mode. In love the rift between reason and inclination disappears,[6] and in love all thought of duty vanishes. This does not mean that Jesus abolishes law: 'Think not that I am come to destroy the law, or the prophets: I am not come to destroy but to fulfil' (Matthew 5: 17). But the fulfilment announced by Jesus transcends mere obedience to the law of reason: 'For I say unto you, That except your righteousness shall exceed the righteousness of the scribes and Pharisees, ye shall in no case enter into the kingdom of heaven' (Matthew 5: 20). This new righteousness, Hegel says, 'we may call an inclination so to act as the laws may command, i.e., a unification of inclination with the law *whereby the latter loses its form as law*'. The 'ought' becomes an 'is'[7] – and the 'is' is the synthesis of subject and object, in which they have lost their opposition 'while in the Kantian conception of virtue this opposition remains, and the universal becomes the master and the particular the mastered'. Law and inclination no longer merely 'correspond': they are simply one. Take for example the command 'Thou shalt not kill.' Such a maxim is recognized as valid for the will of every rational being, and valid as a principle of universal legislation. But against such a command 'Jesus sets the higher genius of reconcilability (a modification of love) which not only does not act counter to this law but makes it wholly superfluous.... In reconcilability the law loses its form, the concept is displaced by life.'[8]

The ideas first adumbrated in these passages of *The Spirit of Christianity* were to remain absolutely fundamental to Hegel's social and political thought. From the Frankfurt period onwards he was to widen and deepen his objections to what in *The Phenomenology of Mind* he was to call 'the moral view of the world' – the view, in other words, that a satisfactory life could be lived by obedience to the dictates of the individual conscience, and from his first published works, *The Difference between the Philosophies of Fichte and Schelling* (1800) and his long article of 1802–3 published in the *Kritisches Journal der Philosophie* (edited by him and Schelling), 'On the Scientific Ways of Dealing with Natural Law', to the last treatise which he published, *The Philosophy of Right*, Hegel was concerned to show the limitations, the self-contradictions and sometimes even the disasters which beset those who seek to govern their lives purely by the dictates of individual conscience, in short to show that individual conscience cannot possibly be on its own a guide to a happy or satisfactory or even a virtuous life.

Morality or the moral view of the world depends on the subjectivity of the will, on the awareness of the subject that his decisions depend not on an outside power, on nature, on tradition, or on God, but on himself. The awareness of subjectivity is a late phenomenon which Hegel says came into the world with Christianity and gradually spread in the modern world, particularly after, and as a consequence of, the

Protestant reformation with its emphasis on the direct relationship between the believer and God, and thus on the importance of conviction and the claims of conscience. And it is Kant's achievement, and after him that of Fichte, to have seen clearly and to have described rigorously the character and conditions of moral action. To say that will is subjective is to say that its determinations – or indetermination – are a matter for itself, and not for any power or influence outside itself.

> The will contains [α] the element of pure indeterminacy or that pure reflection of the ego into itself which involves the dissipation of every restriction and every content either immediately presented by nature, by needs, desires, and impulses, or given and determined by any means whatever.[9]

This awareness by the subject that his will can dissipate all restrictions whatever leads to what Hegel calls the process of vaporization:

> This subjectivity, *qua* abstract self-determination and pure certainty of oneself alone, [as readily] evaporates into itself the whole determinate character of right, duty, and existence, as it remains both the power to judge, to determine from within itself alone, what is good in respect of any content.[10]

Hegel discusses (both in *The Phenomenology* and in *The Philosophy of Right*) the historical conditions under which this process of vaporization takes place. As one of the commoner features of history (for example, in Socrates, the Stoics and others), the tendency to look deeper into oneself and to know and determine from within oneself what is right and good appears in ages when what is recognized as right and good in contemporary manners cannot satisfy the will of better men:

> It is only in times when the world of actuality is hollow, spiritless, and unstable, that an individual may be allowed to take refuge from actuality in his inner life. His thought vaporized the world around him and he withdrew into himself to search there for the right and the good.[11]

What is the outcome of this vaporization?

> Once self-consciousness has reduced all otherwise valid duties to emptiness and itself to sheer inwardness of the will it has become the potentiality of either making the absolutely universal its principle, or equally well of elevating above the universal the self-will of private particularity, taking that as its principle and realizing it through its actions, i.e. it has become potentially evil.[12]
>
> To have a conscience, if conscience is only formal subjectivity, is simply to be on the verge of slipping into evil.[13]

What is vaporized is condensed out again, in new rules and new arrangements which the will finds satisfactory and in which it is at home. But yet there is another possibility, namely that the will refuses to commit itself to any determination, that it remains suspended in indeterminacy, or else that whatever it determines it immediately destroys in the belief that determination is limitation and indeterminacy absolute freedom. This is not a mere academic possibility. 'This negative freedom', as Hegel calls it, is

> the freedom of the void which rises to a passion and takes shape in the world . . . it takes shape in religion as the Hindu fanaticism of pure contemplation . . . but when it turns to actual practice, it takes shape in religion and politics alike as the fanaticism of destruction. . . . Only in destroying something does this negative will possess the feeling of itself as existent. Of course it imagines that it is willing some positive state of affairs,

such as universal equality . . . but in fact it does not will that this shall be positively actualized and for this reason: such actuality leads at once to some sort of order, to a particularization of organizations and individuals alike; while it is precisely out of the annihilation of particularity and objective characterization that the self-consciousness of this negative freedom proceeds.[14]

Hence Hegel connects the quest for absolute freedom with terror.

But there remain the two other cases – the will making private particularity its will – and this is the evil will – and, second, the will making the absolutely universal its principle.

The subjective will seeking to make the universal its principle taken simply as such is an aspiration, a demand, an ought-to-be. It is opposed to objectivity because what is objective is seen not to embody the universal. Subjectivity and objectivity are distinct from one another or united only by their mutual contradiction.[15] In morality, says Hegel, self-determination is to be thought of as the pure restlessness and activity which can never arrive at anything that *is*.

But, it may be objected, Kant does after all tell us what the content of such a will is: so to act that the principle of one's action can be the universal law. This is duty, and a virtuous will is a will which acts from duty. But what does this mean, what does it exactly involve? Hegel objects that to act as if the maxim of your action could be laid down as a universal principle is defective in that it lacks all articulation. If it is to serve as a determinant of universal legislation it must have a content. But Kant's principle does not have a content. It is simply a principle of non-contradiction which is productive of nothing, since 'where there is nothing there can be no contradiction either'.[16]

Kant's doctrine is abstract universality – pure formalism, the preaching of duty for duty's sake. You can bring in a specific content from the outside but if duty is the absence of contradiction then no transition is possible to the specification of particular duties, nor can you have any criteria for deciding whether a specific action is or is not a duty. 'On the contrary, by this means any wrong or immoral line of conduct may be justified.'[17]

There is yet another objection to Kant's doctrine of morality. It is that it establishes a cleavage between happiness and virtue.[18] Men, says Hegel, seek satisfaction in their action. They are willing to be *active* in what interests them, or should interest them. Subjective satisfaction is also part and parcel of the achievement of ends of absolute worth.[19]

But happiness is not freedom. Freedom is not free except in the good, that is, except when it is its own end.

> Consequently we may raise the question whether a man has the right to set before himself ends not freely chosen but resting solely on the fact that the subject is a living being. The fact that man is a living being, however, is not fortuitous, but in conformity with reason, and to that extent he has a right to make his needs his end. There is nothing degrading in being alive, and there is no mode of intelligent being higher than life in which existence would be possible. It is only the raising of the given to something self-created which yields the higher orbit of the good, *although this distinction implies no incompatibility between the two levels.*[20]

As regards the other case of the subjective will – the will making private particularity its will, Hegel considers it in much detail, notably in paragraph 140 of the *Philosophy of Right* with its long remark and addition. The evil will is passed off by the subject as good both in his eyes and in that of others. To impose in this way on others is hypocrisy, while to impose on oneself is a stage beyond hypocrisy, a stage at which subjectivity claims to be absolute. Among these perversions of the will, we may mention here particularly the view that the goodness of the will consists in its willing the good[21] – which in the end does away with the distinction between good and evil,[22] and the view that the conviction which holds something to be right is to decide the ethical character of an action. At this stage hypocrisy is transcended and there is nothing absolutely vicious or criminal – we have instead the man who is fully justified by intention or conviction – sincerity is all. A sincerity issuing in nihilism. You are sincere, I am sincere, everyone is sincere – so who is to judge?

> This type of subjectivism not merely substitutes a void for the whole content of ethics, right, duties, and laws – and so is evil, in fact evil through and through and universally – but in addition its form is a subjective void, i.e. it knows itself as this contentless void and in this knowledge knows itself as absolute.[23]

The life of mere subjectivity is impossible, destructive and self-destructive. These pages of Hegel's (93–103) may be read as the drama of the modern European psyche, with its taste for annihilation and self-annihilation.

More specifically, mere subjectivity cannot possibly serve to make any satisfactory political arrangements – such as would make men feel at home in the world. Its outcome is either anarchy, or despotism, or paralysis. Anarchy if subjectivity is not guided by the universal. But if it is guided by the universal then would supervene the situation which Hegel objected to when he discussed Kant's moral theory in *The Spirit of Christianity*. In such a situation, the subject is divided within himself and there is no coincidence between the will and the universal.[24] The empirical self must be transformed into the rational self.[25] Who is to do the transforming? The government? But this is composed of empirical selves who themselves have to be controlled by those over whom they rule. This leads to deadlock. Or, the universal is what the rulers lay down – and then men are forced to be free. This is a paradox which has two consequences: (a) The government must in the end resort to minute regulation of all activities to see that the universal is not infringed – see Fichte's *Closed Commercial State*, 1800, and (b) anyway the universal can never be realized. The injunction to help the poor must mean that poverty should be abolished. However, the maxim as a universal maxim requires that there should always be poor to help (otherwise the maxim is impossible to realize) or that all should be poor (which makes the maxim meaningless).[26]

Ideological politics leads to contradictions. But the question then arises, are there any politics which in the modern world can escape such contradictions?

### Notes

1 Knox and Kroner, pp. 70–1.
2 Asveld, p. 67.
3 *The Spirit of Christianity and its Fate* is in Knox and Kroner, p. 253.
4 Knox and Kroner, p. 211.
5 Ibid., p. 212.
6 Ibid., p. 213.
7 Ibid., p. 214.
8 Ibid., p. 215.
9 *Hegel's Philosophy of Right*, trans. with notes by T. M. Knox (Oxford, Oxford University Press, 1945), para 5.
10 Ibid., para 138.
11 Ibid., para 138A.
12 Ibid., para 139.
13 Ibid., para 139R.

14 Ibid., para 5R.
15 Ibid., paras 108, 108A, 112R.
16 Ibid., para 135A.
17 Ibid., para 153.
18 Ibid., paras 123, 124.
19 Point raised in *Spirit of Christianity* in Knox and Kroner.
20 *Phil of Right*, para 123A.
21 Ibid., pp. 96–7.
22 Ibid., pp. 98–9.
23 Ibid., pp. 102–3.
24 Hegel, essay on *Natural Law*.
25 Criticism of Fichte.
26 G. W. F. Hegel, *Le Droit naturel*, translated from the German with a preface and annotations by André Kaan (Paris, Editions Gallimard, 1972), p. 96.

# 9
# PROPERTY AND PERSONALITY

If Athens is dead and gone, if love is inefficacious, if individual conscience is a treacherous and occasionally disastrous guide, can we find a principle in the mind of man which in its development will enable him to build for himself a world in which he will feel at home? It is man with his mind and will – and who says man says mind, and who says mind says will – who constitutes the active principle in the world; it is his activities which make the world in which he recognizes himself to be at home. To use an expression of Dilthey's, a successor of Hegel's in the Berlin chair of philosophy, the world is a mind-affected world. In the second series of Hegel's Iena lectures, the *Realphilosophie* of 1805–6, there is a remarkable passage in which he tries to describe the power, the originating, creative and destructive powers, of the mind. Hegel says:

> Man is this night, this empty nothingness, which in its simplicity contains everything: a wealth of an infinite number of representations and images, none of which emerges at a precise moment in his spirit, or which are not always present. It is night, the intimacy of nature which exists here: *pure self*. There is night all around the fantastic representations: here emerges a bloody head, there a white figure; and just as suddenly they disappear.

It is this night which you see when you look a man in the eyes: you plunge then into a night which becomes *terrible*; it is the night of the world which now faces us.[1]

The power to draw images out of this night or to drop them back into it, this is the act of self-positing, internal consciousness, action, scission. It is into this night that being has withdrawn; but the movement of this power is equally posited.

When the movement of this power is inward, what we have is the endless confrontation of subjectivity with itself, the drama of the individual conscience like the Young Fate in Valéry's poem[2] – a Hegelian poem:

> I ask my heart what pain keeps it awake,
> What crime committed against me or by myself? . . .
> . . . . . . . . . . . . . . . . . . . .
> I saw me seeing myself, sinuous, and
> From gaze to gaze gilded my innermost forests.
> I was tracking a snake there that had just stung me.

But the movement of this power is also outward. In this case the self finds itself standing over against a natural world, external and objective. This relationship is one of confrontation. Its first and most primitive form is desire or appetite which feels satisfaction simply by obliterating the object of desire. Eating may stand here as an example of this simple obliteration. But immediate desire can also be suppressed, its satisfaction postponed and obtained through labour. This desire or appetite the satisfaction of which is mediated through labour is a peculiarly human desire. Of man confronting nature and working on it to satisfy his desire by possession or modification, Hegel says that he is a *person*:

> Personality implies that as *this* person (i) I am completely determined on every side (in my inner caprice, impulse, and desire, as well as by immediate external facts) and so

finite, yet (ii) none the less . . . I know myself as something infinite, universal and free.³

A person confronts the world of nature: the subjective confronting the objective. Therefore

> For personality . . . as inherently infinite and universal, the *restriction of being only subjective* is a contradiction and a nullity. Personality *is that which struggles to lift itself above this restriction and to give itself reality*, or in other words to claim that *external world as its own.*⁴

If man is to be conscious of his power and to realize it – and this is what to be at home in the world, and to be free, means – he must translate it into an external sphere, he must objectify it. This goes beyond the satisfaction of animal desires. To possess something is to begin to realize one's freedom:

> The rationale of property is to be found not in the satisfaction of needs but in the supersession of the pure subjectivity of personality.⁵

Again:

> If emphasis is placed on my needs, then the possession of property appears as a means to their satisfaction, but the true position is that, from the standpoint of freedom, property is the first embodiment of freedom and so is in itself a substantive end.⁶

Or again:

> The fact that property is realized and actualized only in use floats before the minds of those who look upon property as derelict and a *res nullius* if it is not being put to any use, and who excuse its unlawful occupancy on the ground that it has not been used by its owner. But the owner's will . . . is the primary substantive basis of property; use is a further modification of property . . . ⁷

This way of looking at property, as a means of escaping from the restriction of subjectivity, leads Hegel to a criticism of Plato's *Republic,* which he considered to be 'in essence nothing but an interpretation of the nature of Greek ethical life':[8]

> The general principle that underlies Plato's ideal state violates the right of personality by forbidding the holding of private property. The idea of a pious or friendly and even a compulsory brotherhood of men holding their goods in common and rejecting the principle of private property may readily present itself to the disposition which mistakes the true nature of the freedom of mind.[9]

Hegel cites Epicurus who, when his 'friends proposed to form such an association holding goods in common, he forbade them, precisely on the ground that their proposal betrayed distrust and that those who distrusted each other were not friends'.

This passage occurs in *The Philosophy of Right*, that is, it comes towards the end of Hegel's career. But his preoccupation with the significance of property for human self-realization and human freedom is apparent as early as the Frankfurt period. In *The Spirit of Christianity and its Fate* he quotes Matthew 19: 23, 'How hard it is for a rich man to enter the Kingdom of Heaven,' and comments that about it 'there is nothing to be said; it is a litany pardonable only in sermons and rhymes, for such a command is without truth for us. The fate of property has become too powerful to tolerate reflections on it, to find its abolition thinkable.'[10]

Again, in another essay dating from 1800, of which only a fragment has survived, Hegel discusses the significance of religious sacrifices. Religion is absolute union between the worshipper and his God. But if the worshipper retains things in his grasp he 'would not yet have fulfilled the negative prerequisites of religion, i.e. would not yet be free from absolute objectivity and would not yet have risen above finite life',[11] and this because

> he would have kept something for himself; he would still be in a state of mastering things or caught in a dependence upon them. This is the reason why he gives up only part of his property as a sacrifice, for it is *his fate to possess property, and this fate* is necessary and can never be discarded. . . . The destruction of property [on the altar] is . . . [a] negation of private ownership because such destruction is useless and superfluous. . . . This aimless destruction for destruction's sake . . . proves to be the only religious relation to absolute objects.

Again in an essay on *Love* which dates from late 1797 or early 1798, that is, from before *The Spirit of Christianity*, Hegel discusses private property and love. The union of lovers, he says, is complete

> but it can remain so only as long as the separate lovers are opposed solely in the sense that the one loves and the other is loved. . . . Yet the lovers are in connection with much that is dead; external objects belong to each of them. . . . this is why lovers are capable of a multiplex opposition in the course of their multiplex acquisition and possession of property and rights. The dead object in the power of one of the lovers is opposed to both of them, and a union in respect of it seems to be possible only if it comes under the dominion of both. The one who sees the other in possession of a property must sense in the other the separate individuality which has willed this possession. . . . *Since possession and property make up such an important part of men's life, cares, and thoughts, even lovers cannot refrain from reflection on this aspect of their relations.* Even if the use of property is common to both, the right to its possession would remain undecided, and the thought of this right, would

never be forgotten, because everything which men possess has the legal form of property.[12]

If it is man's fate to possess property, and if this fate is necessary (to adopt Hegel's formulation in the essay of 1800), then not only the subjective life but also the life of love (whether sacred or profane) are both likely to prove unsatisfactory, and so also would be the life of the polis in which all property was at the disposal of the polis – of which Plato's *Republic* is the philosophical mirror.

We have to notice one other consideration which Hegel brings forward in regard to property. The important thing about property, Hegel remarks, is that I possess it,[13]

> but the particular aspect comprises subjective aims, needs, arbitrariness, abilities, external circumstances and so forth. On these mere possession as such depends. . . . What and how much I possess, therefore, is a matter of indifference so far as rights are concerned.

Possession, remarks Hegel, is 'this terrain of inequality'. It is misconceived to ask for equality of possessions:

> The equality which might be set up, e.g. in connection with the distribution of goods, would all the same soon be destroyed again, because wealth depends on diligence. But if a project cannot be executed, it ought not to be executed. Of course men are equal, but only *qua* persons, that is, with respect to the source from which possession springs; the inference from this is that everyone must have property. Hence, if you wish to talk of equality, it is this equality which you must have in view. But this equality is something apart from the fixing of particular amounts, from the question of how much I own. . . . particularity is just the sphere where there is room for inequality and where equality would be wrong.

Hegel warns against confusing property and the need for subsistence:

> That everyone ought to have subsistence enough for his needs is a moral wish and thus vaguely expressed is well enough meant, but like anything that is only well meant it lacks objectivity. . . . subsistence is not the same as possession and belongs to another sphere, i.e. to civil society.

What Hegel means by civil society and its relation to property we shall consider in due course. Here we have to distinguish between two terms which Hegel uses: namely *property* and *possession*.

> We take possession of a thing [α] by directly grasping it physically, [β] by forming it, [γ] by merely marking it as ours.[14]

But possessing a thing is not enough to make it my property:

> Since property is the *embodiment* of personality, my inward idea and will that something is to be mine is not enough to make it my property. . . . The embodiment which my willing thereby attains involves its *recognizability* by others.[15]

What is the significance of the recognizability and what does it entail?

> All things may become man's property, because man is free will and consequently is absolute. . . . Thus everyone has the right to make his will the thing or to make the thing his will, or in other words to destroy the thing and transform it into his own . . . . Thus 'to appropriate' means at bottom only to manifest the pre-eminence of my will over the thing and to prove that it is not absolute, is not an end in itself. . . . The free will, therefore, is the idealism which does not take things as they are to be absolute, while realism pronounces them

## Property and Personality

to be absolute, even if they only exist in the form of finitude. Even an animal has gone beyond this realist philosophy since it devours things and so proves that they are not absolutely self-subsistent.[16]

If a thing is my property, it is because I have put my free will into it; but it can happen that someone else also has put his free will into it. Here then is a dispute which involves superficially the possession of the thing, but in reality involves the *recognition* of my right by another. If there is recognition then possession does become property. If there is challenge, what the challenge involves is not mere possession of a mere thing; it is in reality a struggle between two free wills, a struggle implicating the totality of their being, a struggle which in the absence of laws and political institutions becomes a struggle to the death.

This struggle may result in the death of one or of both of the contestants. In this case no further problem remains. But should one of the contestants lose his nerve, flinch and give way, then a new situation arises, in which the cause of the quarrel, namely the right of property in an object, retreats into the background, and the two contestants now establish a relationship of master and slave. This relationship and its dialectic Hegel explores in some of the most brilliant pages of the *Phenomenology of Mind*, a dialectic which has far-reaching implications for his view of labour and its place in the human creation of freedom, of a world in which man can feel at home. How has the master become a master?

> It is solely by risking life that freedom is obtained; only thus is it tried and proved that the essential nature of self-consciousness is not bare existence . . . is not its mere absorption in the expanse of life. . . . The individual who has not staked his life, may, no doubt, be recognized as a

Person; but he has not attained the truth of this recognition as an independent self-consciousness.[17]

The victor, on the other hand, the master, 'is the consciousness that exists *for itself*'; but this consciousness that exists *for itself* so exists as 'mediated with itself through an other consciousness, i.e. through an other whose very nature implies that it is bound up with an independent being or with thinghood in general [i.e. the slave].'[18]

'Since he is the power dominating existence, while this existence again is the power controlling the other [the slave], the master holds ... this other in subordination ... the master relates himself to the thing mediately through the slave ... the slave merely works on the thing.' The master gets the enjoyment. 'What mere desire did not attain, he now succeeds in attaining . . . [to] find satisfaction in enjoyment.'[19]

> Desire alone did not get the length of this, because of the independence of the thing. The master, however, who has interposed the slave between it and himself, thereby relates himself merely to the dependence of the thing, and enjoys it without qualification and without reserve. The aspect of its independence he leaves to the slave, who labours upon it.[20]

The slave and the master have a new relationship – a one-sided and unequal relationship. But in his very mastery, the master finds that he is dependent for his enjoyment on the work of his slave.

The master is 'thus not assured of self-existence as his truth; he finds that his truth is rather the unessential consciousness, and the fortuitous unessential action of that consciousness'.[21]

> But just as lordship showed its essential nature to be the reverse of what it wants to be, so, too, bondage will,

when completed, pass into the opposite of what it immediately is: being a consciousness repressed within itself, it will enter into itself, and *change round into real and true independence.*

Through work and labour, this consciousness of the slave comes to itself.

Desire in the master's consciousness 'has reserved to itself the pure negating of the object and thereby unalloyed feeling of self'.

> Labour, on the other hand, is desire restrained and checked, evanescence delayed and postponed; in other words, labour shapes and fashions the thing. The negative relation to the object passes into the *form* of the object, into something that is permanent and remains. . . . This negative mediating agency, this activity giving shape and form . . . now in the work it does is externalized and passes into the condition of permanence.[22]

By his activity the slave

> becomes aware of its own proper negativity, its existence on its own account . . . through the fact that it cancels the actual form confronting it. But this objective negative element is precisely the alien, external reality, before which it trembled. Now . . . it destroys this extraneous alien negative, affirms and sets itself up as a negative . . . , and thereby becomes for itself a self-existent being. . . . in fashioning the thing, self-existence comes to be felt explicitly as his own proper being, and he attains the consciousness that he himself exists in and for himself (*an und für sich*). . . . By the fact that the form is objectified, it does not become something other than the consciousness moulding the thing through work; for just that form is his pure self-existence, which therein becomes truly realized. Thus precisely in labour where there seemed to be merely some outsider's mind and ideas involved, the slave becomes aware, through this

rediscovery of himself by himself of having and being 'a mind of his own'.[23]

Man makes his own world. Is freedom then to come through labour?

### Notes

1. Kostas Papaioannou, *Hegel* (Paris, Editions Seghers, 1962), p. 180.
2. Epigraph from Corneille. 'Did Heaven form this mass of marvels / To be a serpent's dwelling-place?' *Paul Valéry: Poems*, trans. David Paul (London, Routledge & Kegan Paul, 1971), p. 71.
3. *Phil of Right*, para 35.
4. Ibid., para 39.
5. Ibid., para 41A.
6. Ibid., para 45R.
7. Ibid., para 59R.
8. Ibid., Preface p. 10
9. Ibid., para 46R.
10. Knox and Kroner p. 221.
11. Ibid., pp. 315–16.
12. Ibid., p. 308.
13. *Phil of Right*, paras 49R & A.
14. Ibid., para 54.
15. Ibid., para 51.
16. Ibid., para 44A.
17. *Phenomenology of Mind*, p. 233.
18. Ibid., pp. 234–5.
19. Ibid., p. 235.
20. Ibid., pp. 235–6.
21. Ibid., p. 237.
22. Ibid., p. 238.
23. Ibid., p. 239.

# 10

# LABOUR AND CIVIL SOCIETY

By the time that Hegel came to write his passage on the relation between the master and the servant in *The Phenomenology of Mind*, the evidence shows that he had already devoted a great deal of thought to the character and significance of labour and to the distinguishing features of modern industrial economics. His lectures at Iena show that he had studied Adam Smith, but we also know that economic issues, along with political and theological ones, were at the centre of his preoccupations in the extraordinarily fruitful and formative Frankfurt period. For along with the *Spirit of Christianity and its Fate* which he wrote then (and which, as I mentioned in my last lecture has a very suggestive reference to property and wealth), and the writing, parts of which have survived, which has been entitled 'Fragment of a System' (which also contains allusions to property), as well as the long and important essay entitled by his editors *The German Constitution*, most of which he seems to have written in Frankfurt, Hegel also wrote a long commentary on a work about economics. This commentary is now lost and is known only from the references to it which occur in Rosenkrantz's biography, published in 1844. The work to which this commentary was devoted was Sir James

Steuart's *Inquiry into the Principles of Political Oeconomy*, first published in 1767, and published in two different German translations, 1769–1772.[1] Though Hegel does not refer to Steuart in those writings of his which have survived, the Scots writer's influence on him, as the French scholar Paul Chamley has exhaustively demonstrated, was enormous and perhaps crucial.

In his treatise, Steuart, as his title-page informs us, proposes to consider particularly 'Population, agriculture, trade, industry, money, coin, interest, circulation, banks, exchange, public credit, and taxes'. From this list we see that Steuart, though he is concerned (in the last three books of his work) with technical questions relating to money and public finance, is also much interested in wider issues (which he discusses in the first two books), the issues which he lists under the headings: population, agriculture, trade, industry. In fact, if we examine the first two books of the *Inquiry* we discover that Steuart is engaged in nothing less than a historical inquiry the purpose of which is to show how men's government and their manner of satisfying their needs are connected with one another, and under what influences, and in what manner, government and economic activity undergo change.

Though Steuart starts from the common assumption of the Enlightenment that there is a uniform human nature which is subject to uniformity and uniform laws, yet he is also very much impressed by the way in which these uniform laws produce diverse social and political conditions:

> Man we find acting *uniformly* in all ages, in all countries, and in all climates from the principles of self-interest, expediency, duty, or passion. In this he is alike, in nothing else.

## Labour and Civil Society 117

These motives of human actions produce such a *variety* of circumstances, that if we consider the several species of animals in the creation, we shall find the individuals of no class so unlike to one another, as man to man.[2]

Steuart's purpose in his first two books and his historical vision are very well illustrated by a passage which occurs in chapter II of book I:

If governments be taken in general, we shall find them analogous to the spirit of the people. But the point under consideration is, how a statesman is to proceed, when expediency and refinement require a change of administration, or when it becomes necessary from a change of circumstances.

The great alteration in the affairs of Europe within these three centuries, by the discovery of America and the Indies, the springing up of industry and learning, the introduction of trade and the luxurious arts, the establishment of public credit, and a general system of taxation, have entirely altered the plan of government every where.

From feudal and military, it is become free and commercial. I oppose freedom in government to the feudal system, to mark only that there is not found now that chain of subordination among the subjects, which made the essential part of the feudal form. The head there had little power, and the lower classes of the people little liberty. Now every industrious man, who lives with oeconomy, is free and independent under most forms of government. Formerly, the power of the barons swallowed up the independency of all inferior classes. I oppose commercial to military, because the military governments now are made to subsist from the consequences and effects of commerce only: that is, from the revenue of the state, proceeding from taxes. Formerly, everything was brought about by numbers; now, numbers of men cannot be kept together without money.[3]

As we see from this passage, Steuart is very much alive to social and economic change: 'From feudal and military, it is become free and commercial.' And his work seeks to find *how exactly* the feudal and military does become the free and commercial. Steuart seems to believe that the mainspring of historical change lies in economic activity: 'the regular progress of mankind, from great simplicity to complicated refinement'. In the first book he sets out 'with taking up society in the cradle, as I may say'. He examines here 'the principles' which influence 'the multiplication' of mankind, 'the method of providing for their subsistence, the origin of their labour, the effects of their liberty and slavery, the distribution of them into classes'. He promises to disclose 'the principles of industry influencing the multiplication of mankind, and the cultivation of the soil': 'This I have thrown in on purpose to prepare my reader for the subject of the second book, where he will find the same principle (under the wings of liberty) providing an easy subsistence for a numerous populace, by the means of trade, which sends the labour of an industrious people over the whole world.'[4]

'The regular progress of mankind' is regular because history is not a mere 'tissue of contingencies'. Not a mere tissue of contingencies because the development of society is governed by two factors: (a) that man is dominated by sexual desire which results in pushing up population to the supply of food at any given time; and (b) that man is moved by self-interest or self-love. Using these two postulates, Steuart explains the particular form of any given society and how its own development compels it to change its economic organization, its culture and the idea of human nature it presupposes. Steuart considers three basic types of society, each emerging out of the other: pre-agrarian pastoral societies, agrarian society, and the exchange economy of commercial society.

In pastoral pre-agrarian society men do not labour, but live on the spontaneous fruit of the earth at no more than subsistence level. They lead a nomadic life because there is no cultivation. In this state each man conceives of himself as a free and independent being 'remaining free from every constraint'.

But man could not long remain at this level of material existence. There follows a transition to a labouring agrarian society. Sexual drive leads to reproduction: self-love drives men to secure subsistence for their children. This is incompatible with the maintenance of pre-agrarian economy. In such a situation food is strictly limited to what is available for spontaneous consumption. To secure food for their children, those who had the physical power would try to appropriate part of the land to work it and make it produce more. The agrarian economy thus comes into being and produces a decisive difference between those who can appropriate and those who do not have the power to appropriate land. These latter become the servants, and then the slaves, of the landowners.

Self-love accounts also for the change to modern commercial society. Labouring on the soil produces a surplus beyond what is necessary for consumption. This surplus is used to barter for commodities which the owner of the surplus desires. This generates its own momentum. Men work harder to produce more surplus to acquire more commodities – men thus become slaves to their wants. Trade and industry are the result, and slavery becomes an outmoded form of economic relation. This is because slavery is incompatible with the free competition necessary for the development of industry: slaves are cheaper than free men and their labour will depress industry. (Some writers have applied this argument to the American South, and *mutatis mutandis* to South Africa, and to account for the inferior productivity of socialist economies.) The master–slave relation gives way to a complex web of mutual interdependence. Exchange economy is accompanied by an increase in urbanization and there comes to be a society which is 'a general, tacit contract from which reciprocal and proportional services result universally between all those who compose it'.[5]

It is worthwhile dwelling on some of the aspects of this society of mutual interdependence as Steuart sees them. For Steuart, this society produced a spontaneous order of its own: 'The whole magic of a well-ordered society is that each man works for others, while believing that he is working for himself.'[6]

Another way of making the same point is his contrast between ancient luxury and modern. Ancient luxury is built on the assertion of power, modern on exchange.

> the punic wars exalted the grandeur of plundering Rome, and blotted out the existence of industrious Carthage. . . .
>
> Ancient luxury was quite *arbitrary*; consequently could be laid under no limitations, but produced the worst effects, which *naturally* and *mechanically* could proceed from it.
>
> Modern luxury is *systematical*; it cannot make one step, but at the expense of an adequate equivalent, acquired by those who stand the most in need of the protection and assistance of their fellow-citizens; and without producing a vibration in the balance of their wealth.[7]

The exchange economy, again, by its very complexity, limits and moderates political power:

> I deduce the origin of the great subordination under the feudal government, from the necessary dependence of the lower classes for their subsistence. They consumed the produce of the land, as the price of their

# Labour and Civil Society

subordination, not as the reward of their industry in making it produce.

I deduce modern liberty from the independence of the same classes, by the introduction of industry, and circulation of an adequate equivalent for every service.[8] . . .

When once a state begins to subsist by the consequences of industry, there is less danger to be apprehended from the power of the sovereign. The mechanism of his administration becomes more complex and . . . he finds himself so bound up by the laws of his political oeconomy that every transgression of them runs him into new difficulties. . . .

The Lacedemonian form [of government] may be compared to the wedge, the most solid and compact of all the mechanical powers. Those of modern states to watches, which are continually going wrong; sometimes the spring is found too weak, at other times too strong for the machine . . . then the machine stops, and if it be forced, some part gives way; and the workman's hand becomes necessary to set it right.[9]

One last point made by Steuart is worth noticing. He declares 'Were public spirit, instead of private utility, to become the spring of action in the individuals of a well-governed state, I apprehend it would spoil all.'

Public spirit is something necessary in the rulers but 'superfluous' in the ruled: 'every man is to act for his own interest in what regards the public; and politically speaking, everyone ought to do so.'

'You must love your country. Why? Because it is *yours*. But you must not prefer your own interest to that of your country.' But this only means that you should abstain from unlawful gain, as for example by selling state secrets to a foreign power. But

Were the principle of public spirit carried farther; were a people to become quite disinterested, there would be no possibility of governing them. Every one might consider the interest of his country in a different light, and many might join in the ruin of it, by endeavouring to promote its advantages. Were a rich merchant to begin and sell his goods without profit, what would become of trade? Were another to defray the extraordinary expense of some workmen in a hard year, in order to enable them to carry on their industry, without raising their price, what would become of others, who had not the like advantages? Were a man of a large landed estate to sell his grain at a low price in a year of scarcity, what would become of the poor farmers? Were the people to feed all who would ask charity, what would become of industry?[10]

As Chamley has shown, there can be little doubt that Hegel was profoundly influenced by Steuart's work, and influenced in at least two ways. From the Frankfurt period onwards Hegel has a lively sense that *Geist*, 'mind' or 'spirit', works itself out, finds and knows itself through its own activity, over time, that *Geist* is the history of its own acts. This is the basis of his criticism of Christian love as a way of life. As we have seen, he calls it an unliving love. In a passage which comes immediately before, he explains why a society based on this exclusive all-embracing love is bound to fail:

> In love man has found himself again in another. Since love is a unification of life, it presupposes division, a development of life, a developed many-sidedness of life. The more variegated the manifold in which life is alive, the more places in which it can be reunified.

But a community bound by love must be small and isolated. A large group of people cannot be united by love but only by needs. This linking 'reveals itself in objects which can be common, in relationships arising from such objects, and then in a common striving for them and a common activity and enterprise'.[11]

In the Iena lectures, the *Realphilosophie*, and in the *Philosophy of Right* Hegel explores the implications of needs, of labouring which satisfies these needs, of the way in which a community of needs gets established – what its limitations are, and how these limitations are overcome and transcended.

The second aspect of Steuart's influence on Hegel lies in this, that Hegel comes to see the coming into being in the modern world of an economic order based on the exchange of commodities, and also comes to see that this is an entirely new development, a feature in fact which distinguishes the modern state from the polis, the watch from the wedge, to use Steuart's imagery. And one of the most original features of the *Philosophy of Right* is the way in which Hegel works out the various political implications of this development.

In the 1805–6 lectures Hegel argues that labour is the outcome of man's confrontation with the natural, the objective, the external world. Labour results in an objectification of man's subjective powers: 'I have done something, I have externalized myself; this negation is positive; externalization is appropriation.'[12]

But this labour, which is based on need, is not labour carried out by a solitary being. It is, and must be, social. Satisfaction of needs leads to exchange and to specialization. Man comes to satisfy his needs 'not through the object which is being worked upon by him'.

> Man does not produce any more that which he needs, nor does he need any more that which he produces.
>
> His labour and his possessions are not what they are for him, but what they are for all. The satisfaction of needs is a universal dependence of all on all; there disappears for everyone the security and the knowledge that his work is immediately adequate to his particular needs; *his* particular need becomes universal.[13]

These needs form 'a system of complete interdependence'[14] – what Hegel in the *Philosophy of Right* calls the civil society. Civil society, says Hegel, is the achievement of the modern world.[15] It is the

> territory of mediation where there is free play for every idiosyncrasy, every talent, every accident of birth and fortune, and where waves of every passion gush forth, regulated only by reason glinting through them.[16]...
>
> The fact that I must direct my conduct by reference to others introduces here the form of universality. It is from others that I acquire the means of satisfaction and I must accordingly accept their views. At the same time, however, I am compelled to produce means for the satisfaction of others. We play into each other's hands and so hang together. To this extent everything private becomes something social.[17]

This system of needs has something anarchic about it: 'The satisfaction of need, necessary and accidental alike, is accidental because it breeds new desires without end, is in thoroughgoing dependence on caprice and external accident.'[18] The satisfaction of individual needs promotes equality. Judy O'Grady and the Colonel's Lady both buy their tights at Marks and Spencer's.

The satisfaction of needs both anarchic and egalitarian works to promote human freedom, the 'liberation intrinsic to work'.[19] Man consumes increasingly the products of the efforts of fellow men. The necessity for these products promotes education, which 'consists in possessing not simply a multiplicity of ideas and facts, but also a flexibility and rapidity of mind, ability to pass from one idea to another; to grasp complex and general relations, and so on'.[20]

The 'restless system of human needs'[21] thus has reason immanent in it. Labour creates 'a universal permanent capital which gives each the opportunity, by the exercise of his education and skill, to draw a share from it, and so be assured of his livelihood, while what he thus earns by means of his work maintains and increases the general capital'.[22]

The system of needs and the means of their satisfaction creates 'means and types of work relative to these needs, modes of satisfaction and of theoretical and practical education, i.e. into systems, to one or other of which individuals are assigned – in other words, into class-divisions'.[23] Civil society and class divisions entail one another. This class-division is not a matter of birth (as in the Indian caste system) or assignment by the rulers (as in Plato's *Republic*): 'The essential and final determining factors are subjective opinion and the individual's arbitrary will.' But this arbitrariness and subjectivity go hand in hand with an objective order. Subjective and objective support one another:

> When subjective particularity is upheld by the objective order in conformity with it and is at the same time allowed its rights, then it becomes the animating principle of the entire civil society, of the development alike of mental activity, merit and dignity. *The recognition and the right that what is brought about by reason of necessity in civil society... shall at the same time be effected by the mediation of the arbitrary will is the more precise definition of what is primarily meant by freedom in common parlance.*[24]

The development and growth of civil society leads to the expectation by everyone that the satisfactions which they seek will be possible of attainment without hindrance.[25] Civil society is a very powerful force. It 'tears the individual away from his family ties, estranges the members of the family from one another, and recognizes them as self-subsistent persons'.[26] And 'the individual becomes a son of civil society which has as many claims upon him as he has rights against it.'

In this civil society composed of self-subsistent persons, membership of a class is a matter of accident, caprice, preference. Taken on his own this self-subsistent individual becomes a solitary, a cypher, a member of a lonely crowd trying 'to gain recognition for himself, by giving external proof of success in his business, *and to these proofs no limits can be set*. He cannot live in the manner of his class, for no class really exists for him.'[27]

The development of civil society produces other evils. Men are free to follow their avocations in civil society – but the situation in which they find themselves may not be of their own creation: 'factors grounded in external circumstances may reduce men to poverty.' The poor are the responsibility of civil society which by its logic has broken down the family and the poor find themselves deprived of 'all the advantages of society, of the opportunity of acquiring skill or education of any kind'.[28]

Again, civil society thrives by specialization and division of labour which produces a surplus of wealth. But the other side of the picture is 'the subdivision and restriction of particular jobs. This results in the dependence and distress of the class tied to work of that sort.'[29] Hegel was early impressed by the dehumanizing effect of factory labour: in his Iena lectures of 1803–4 he wrote that

> the value of labour decreases in the same proportions as the productivity of labour increases. Work becomes thus absolutely more and more dead, it becomes machine-labour, the individual's own skill becomes infinitely limited, and the consciousness of the factory worker is degraded to the utmost level of dullness. The connection between the particular sort of labour and the infinite mass of needs becomes wholly imperceptible, turns into

a blind dependence. It thus happens that a far-away operation often affects a whole class of people who have hitherto satisfied their needs through it; all of a sudden it limits (their work), makes it redundant and useless.[30]

The highest abstraction of labour reaches into the most particular types of labour and thus receives an ever-widening scope. This inequality of wealth and poverty, this need and necessity, turn into the utmost tearing up of the will, an inner indignation and hatred.[31]

Indignation produces a rabble which is 'created only when there is joined to poverty a disposition of mind, an inner indignation against the rich, against society, against the government etc.' Poverty has claims against a society which has called it into being – poverty in civil society is a 'wrong done by one class to another'.[32]

More and more people are involved in this activity, and by its inner dialectic civil society is driven to establish overseas markets and led to embark on colonizing activities overseas.[33] This civil society becomes, says Hegel in his 1803–4 lectures, 'an immense system of community and mutual dependence, a life which is self-moving with a dead reality, a life which in its movement, is agitated in a blind and primitive manner, and which, like a savage beast, needs to be continuously tamed and sternly mastered'.[34]

Hegel's energetically innovative economic thought.

See, for instance, P. Chamley, *Economie Politique et Philosophie chez Stewart et Hegel*, Paris, 1963, pp. 54–5: dialectic of needs – demonstration effect. Dialectic of needs and production – 'dependence effect'. 'Alienation' made popular by Marxism. Under-consumption, concentration of capital, overseas markets, overseas colonization and settlement, civil society a system of needs – general equilibrium theory. Theory of technical progress – 'creative destruction'. Productivity of capital.

Independent search for gain indirectly causes damage – external diseconomies.

Labour a liberation – but labouring in creating this exchange economy has created a 'wild beast' which it cannot itself tame.

Alike with individual conscience, economic activity leads not to freedom but to an impasse.

What is the way out?

**Notes**

1. Sir James Steuart (1713–80) lived in exile from 1745 to 1771.
2. Sir James Steuart, *An Inquiry into the Principles of Political Oeconomy*, edited with an introduction by Andrew S. Skinner (2 vols., Edinburgh and London, 1966), Bk I, ch. I, p. 20. All quotes are from vol. I.
3. Ibid., Bk I, ch. II, p. 24.
4. Ibid., Bk I, ch II, pp. 28–9.
5. Ibid., Bk I, ch. XIV, p. 88.
6. Ibid., p. lxix, footnote 58; Quesnai, *Philosophie rurale*. (Reference untraced – Eds.)
7. Ibid., Bk II, ch. XXII, p. 281.
8. Ibid., Bk II, ch. XIII, pp. 208–9.
9. Ibid., Bk II, ch. XIII, p. 217.
10. Ibid., Bk II, Introduction, pp. 143–4.
11. Knox and Kroner, pp. 278–9.
12. See Shlomo Avineri, 'Labour, Alienation, and Social Classes in Hegel's *Realphilosophie*' in *The Legacy of Hegel: Proceedings of the Marquette Hegel Symposium 1970* (The Hague, Martinus Nijhoff, 1973), p. 201.
13. *Realphilosophie I*; Avineri, *Legacy*, p. 203.
14. *Phil of Right*, para 183.
15. See 'System of needs', *Phil of Right*, para 126.
16. *Phil of Right*, para 182A.
17. Ibid., para 192A.
18. Ibid., para 185.
19. Ibid., para 194R.
20. Ibid., para 197.
21. Ibid., para 200R.
22. Ibid., para 199.
23. Ibid., para 201.

24 See Ibid., para 206 & R.
25 See Ibid., para 234.
26 Ibid., para 238.
27 Ibid., para 253R.
28 Ibid., para 241.
29 Ibid., para 243.
30 *Realphilosophie I*; Avineri, *Legacy* p. 203.
31 *Realphilosophie II*; Avineri, *Legacy* p. 206.
32 *Phil of Right*, para 244A.
33 See Ibid., para 246.
34 I a Ière Phil. 129. (Reference as found – Eds.)

# 11

# CIVIL SOCIETY

The pursuit of universal moral laws does not give man freedom and the certainty of being at home in the world. Love likewise will prove a broken reed. Labour liberates but the liberation intrinsic to labour has many lacks and imperfections, and the world which man creates through his labour proves in the end to be an unsatisfactory world in which men whether rich or poor feel unfree, and moreover strangers in the world which their own labour has created. In the *Phenomenology of Mind* Hegel gave a powerful account (albeit in general terms) of the satisfactions and dissatisfactions created by labouring – alike for those who labour and those who enjoy the fruit of labour. I am referring here of course to the famous dialectic of master and servant which I had occasion to discuss in an earlier lecture.

As we have also seen in his earlier Iena lectures, Hegel had a great deal to say about labour and the benefits and problems which arise out of the organization of labour and economic activities in the new industrial world which Hegel with remarkable acuteness discerned – remarkable because when he put down his reflections on the subject, say between 1800 and 1806, there was very little indeed in the way of modern industry in the German-speaking world, and because even where modern industrial organization had taken root, namely

England, the dialectic inherent in this new kind of activity was apparent to very few, if indeed it was apparent at all.

But it is in his course on *The Philosophy of Right* which he gave in Berlin for the first time in 1818, and which he published in 1820, that Hegel worked out in detail the lineaments and characteristics of what he called civil society (*bürgerliche Gesellschaft*).[1] The great originality of Hegel here is twofold. He sees in the first place that the existence of this civil society differentiates decisively modern society from all societies that have preceded it, and in the second place works out the character and limits of this civil society – its character as something limited, imperfect and ultimately unsatisfactory to the spirit, and its limits which require being transcended – in the life of politics. The life of politics which – albeit in a manner profoundly different from that of the polis – is the only kind of life which can ensure freedom and fulfilment for man.

But limited and finally unsatisfactory as it is, in civil society man has yet fashioned a powerful and sophisticated device to satisfy his needs and enlarge his freedom. Civil society arises out of individual needs and attempts to satisfy them. These attempts cannot succeed except through co-operation in which men become dependent on one another.

> When men are thus dependent on one another and reciprocally related to one another in their work and the satisfaction of their needs, *subjective self-seeking turns into a contribution to the satisfaction of the needs of everyone else.* That is to say, *by a dialectical advance*, subjective self-seeking turns into the mediation of the particular through the universal, with the result that each man in earning, producing, and enjoying on his own account is *eo ipso* producing and earning for the enjoyment of everyone else. The *compulsion* which

brings this about is rooted in the complex interdependence of each on all.²

The civil society which comes about as a result of this dialectic of needs and their satisfaction stands *vis-à-vis* the individual as something very powerful, which exercises mastery over him, and changes him in a radical, far-reaching fashion. The individual comes into existence within a family where he is reared, protected, educated and prepared for adulthood, and then 'civil society *tears* the individual from his family ties, *estranges* the members of the family from one another, and recognizes them as self-subsistent persons. . . . the individual becomes a *son of civil society* which has as many claims upon him as he has rights against it.'³ This society composed of self-subsistent persons tied together by the infinite variety of their needs is, however, nothing arbitrary or despotic. It is a human creation, a creation, in other words, of mind, and thus reason appears in it. 'It is reason, immanent in the *restless* system of *human* needs'⁴ which articulates the society into various groups of suppliers and consumers. In other words 'the restless system of human needs' elicits and brings about an objective and self-sustaining order. It brings about and maintains such an order of itself. The order is not the outcome of despotic power exerted from the outside, but of a multitude of individual decisions freely taken. Hegel remarks that this is very different from ancient society and from Eastern society. In Plato's *Republic* (which Hegel does not consider to be the 'empty ideal' it is commonly taken to be, but 'in essence nothing but an interpretation of the nature of Greek ethical life')⁵ the allotment of individuals to classes is left to the ruling class, while in the Indian caste system it is the outcome of the accident of birth. In these cases 'subjective particularity [is] not incorporated into the organization of society as a whole'[6] and thus any expression of subjective desire would be seen as a corruption and subversion of the social order. This happened in Greece and Rome and, Hegel acutely adds, happens in India today – where these ideas were introduced by European conquerors.

'But when *subjective particularity is upheld by the objective order* in conformity with it and is at the same time allowed its rights, then it becomes the animating principle of the entire civil society, of the *development alike of mental activity, merit and dignity.*' In such a society the subjective and the objective work hand in hand, and not in opposition to one another. A society of this kind is much more stable, because much more satisfying than any other which men have devised: 'The recognition and the right that what is brought about by reason of necessity in civil society and the state shall at the same time be effected by the mediation of the arbitrary will is the more precise definition of what is primarily meant by freedom in common parlance.'[7]

But civil society, the 'restless system of human needs' cannot be a self-sustaining system, and thus cannot be completely satisfactory, and has therefore to be transcended. A market is not a home, and in it you cannot, ultimately, feel fully at home. In the first place, the 'relatedness arising from the reciprocal bearing on one another of needs and work to satisfy these'[8] gives rise to rights, and more specifically to property rights. The safeguard of these rights requires a network of laws and calls for the administration of justice:

> By taking the form of law, right steps into a determinate mode of being. It is then something on its own account, and in contrast with particular willing and opining of the right, it is self-subsistent and has to indicate itself as something universal. This is achieved by recognizing it

and making it actual in a particular case without the subjective feeling of private interest; and this is the business of a *public authority* – the court of justice.[9]

Law and justice are something which a market cannot do without, but also cannot produce on its own, by the dialectic of needs and satisfactions.[10] It requires a 'public authority'. Necessarily implicit in the notion of law is the idea that it is publicly known, and impersonal, that is, applicable without caprice and without regard to particular persons as such. Laws are not arbitrary donations by a ruler. They are 'rational in principle and therefore absolutely necessary'.[11] Again, the administration of justice is 'the fulfilment of duty by the public authority, no less than the exercise of a right'. Hegel denounces vehemently what he describes as a 'barbarous notion', namely that the administration of justice is 'an improper exercise of force, a suppression of freedom, and a despotism'. The notion which Hegel denounces is nowadays known as the theory of institutionalized violence, and we may say that Hegel's remark is one of those (and there are many such in his writings) by which Hegel continually surprises us – surprises us by showing himself to be aware of issues which we are accustomed to think of as peculiarly modern.

One other such remark which Hegel makes *obiter* in *The Philosophy of Right* is to the effect that a bohemian mode of life, the mode of life of hippies and flower people, is 'a rude product of luxury' adding that 'When luxury is at its height, distress and depravity are equally extreme.'[12] Hegel was led to this remark in the course of explaining the increasing sophistication of wants and products which civil society promotes:

> When social conditions tend to multiply and subdivide needs, means, and enjoyments indefinitely . . . this is

luxury. In this same process, however, dependence and want increase *ad infinitum*, and the material to meet these is permanently barred to the needy man.[13]

Civil society, by creating an infinity of wants and a like infinity of ways of satisfying them, creates *ipso facto* social classes to which individuals belong.[14] To which particular class a particular individual belongs 'is one on which natural capacity, birth and other circumstances have their influence, though the essential and final determining factors are subjective opinion and the individual's arbitrary will, which win in this sphere their right, their merit, and their dignity'.[15] Hegel, however, is clear that given a civil society, class divisions have to follow.[16]

Among these classes, which are so to speak the emanation of civil society, one in particular Hegel sees as crucial. This is the class of the poor who are pauperized by the working of civil society itself. The poor may become poor by their own improvidence or lack of abilities, but they are also made poor by external circumstances over which they can have no control.

'When civil society is in a state of unimpeded activity, it is engaged in expanding internally in population and industry.'[17] This increase in wealth takes place through the division of labour – 'the subdivision and restriction of particular jobs. *This results in the dependence and distress of the class tied to work of that sort, and these again entail inability to feel and enjoy the broader freedoms and especially the intellectual benefit of civil society.*' Again, their standard of living may fall below subsistence level. They will not only suffer misery but also the loss of that 'self-respect which makes a man insist on maintaining himself by his own work and effort'.[18]

This results in the creation of a plebs or proletariat (*Pöbel*) full of resentment and ready to rebel. Hegel remarks: 'Poverty in itself does not make men into a *Pöbel*; a *Pöbel* is created when there is joined to poverty a disposition of mind, an inner indignation against the rich, against society, against the government etc.'[19]

This condition is brought about by civil society, and Hegel believes that civil society is unable by its own operation to deal with it. Like justice, this also is the affair of a public authority which transcends the civil society. Hegel is aware that societies have existed in which public organization has claimed to provide for everything and to determine everyone's labour, in which 'the worker's task was not mediated through his private choice and particular interest.'[20] Civil society is at the opposite pole from this – in it there is an immanent tendency to secure freedom of trade and to do away with control from above, but, Hegel observes, 'the more blindly it sinks itself into self-seeking aims, the more it requires such control to bring it back to the universal [and] to diminish the danger of upheavals arising from clashing interests.' Also, since the poor 'still have the needs common to civil society, and yet since society has withdrawn from them the natural means of acquisition ... and broken the bond of the family ... their poverty leaves them more or less deprived of all the advantages of society, of the opportunity of acquiring skill or education of any kind',[21] the public authority must take the place of the family where the poor are concerned.

But of course the poor are not the only class created by civil society. The counterpart of the poor are the rich, and civil society, remarks Hegel, 'brings with it, at the other end of the social scale, conditions which greatly facilitate the concentration of disproportionate wealth in a few hands'.[22] This kind of great wealth which civil society makes possible brings about restlessness, discontent and disorientation. The free-floating self-made millionaire is 'without rank or dignity, his isolation reduces his business to mere self-seeking, and his livelihood and satisfaction become insecure. Consequently, he has to try to gain recognition for himself by giving external proofs of success in his business, *and to these proofs no limits can be set*. He cannot live in the manner of his class, *for no class really exists for him.*' Hegel's observation here is very acute and prophetic. What he describes here is something which has come to be widely remarked in our day, namely the distressful loss of a sense of identity which modern society inflicts on its members, particularly on those who know no other satisfaction than success in competitive economic endeavour. As Hegel points out, no limits can be set to what seems to be required for such a person to feel at home in the world.[23] I would like to quote here a remarkable passage which appeared in the *Daily Telegraph* on 13 March 1976 in which Christopher Booker describes, in an article entitled 'Lost Men of Property', a person such as Hegel had in mind, and the sense of emptiness and insecurity which afflicted him. The man in question was one of those property developers who, from obscure and humble beginnings, have succeeded in making such enormous wealth in this country from the 1960s onwards.

> He told us that he lived in a 'beautiful' Nash house in Regents Park. He told us that one of the reasons why he most liked being a property developer was that he found the history of old buildings he bought so fascinating. . . .
>
> He showed us a book he had written on the history of Lytham St. Annes (which his company owned – the whole town), emphasising the Victorian pictures, and how carefully the town was to be preserved. He proudly announced that he was writing another book on the history of the Port of London Authority headquarters in

Trinity Square, which he had just bought, and that 'His Royal Highness Prince Richard of Gloucester has graciously consented to take the pictures.'. . .

The interview had been altogether an eerie and rather claustrophobic experience – the dominating impression being of a man who, though fabulously rich, was still desperately searching for security, and for recognition of a kind which not all the money in the world could buy.

Is there anything which can be done to cure this distressful condition? Hegel considers that if organizations (which he calls corporations) were to be set up they could perhaps go some way to restoring the sense of identity, of one's place in the world which the civil society has destroyed, and to help those of its members whose livelihood and self-respect civil society has also destroyed. Such a corporation would come on the scene[24] 'like a second family for its members, while civil society can only be an indeterminate sort of family because it comprises everyone and so is farther removed from individuals and their special exigencies'.[25]

Again, 'Within the corporation the help which poverty receives loses its accidental character and the humiliation wrongfully associated with it. The wealthy perform their duties to their fellow associates and thus riches cease to inspire either pride or envy, pride in their owners, envy in others.'[26]

But both corporations and the public authority responsible for justice and the relief of the poor are in the end inadequate, for the end of the corporation is 'restricted and finite'[27] – it is an association for the welfare of producers – while the public authority is 'an external authority involving a separation and a merely relative authority of controller and controlled'. Neither will secure the individual's freedom or enable him to feel at home in the world. The organization which alone can do this is the state. What is the state? It is, says Hegel, 'the actuality of the ethical Idea'.[28] What is the actuality of the living Idea? We may begin by trying to show what it is *not*. The state is not a kind of large family. 'Family piety', says Hegel in passing, 'is feeling, ethical behaviour directed by feeling; political virtue is the willing of the absolute end in terms of thought.'[29] This idea is something which Hegel had worked out as early as the Frankfurt period, in his writing on *The German Constitution*.[30] Hegel is clear that the political tie is not a tie of blood or language:

> In our day the tie between members of a state in respect of manners, education, language may be rather loose or even non-existent. Identity in these matters, once the foundation of a people's union, is now to be reckoned amongst the accidents whose character does not hinder a mass from constituting a public authority. Rome or Athens, like any small modern state, could not have subsisted if the numerous languages current in the Russian Empire had been spoken within their borders, or if amongst their citizens manners had been as different as they are in Russia or, *for that matter, as manners and education are now in every big city in a large country*. Difference in language and dialect . . . , and difference in manners and education in the separate estates which makes men known to one another is hardly anything but outward appearance – such heterogeneous and at the same time most powerful factors the preponderating weight of the Roman Empire's power (once it had become great) was able to overcome and hold together, just as in modern states the same result is produced by *the spirit and art of political institutions. Thus dissimilarity in culture and manners is a necessary product as well as a necessary condition of the stability of modern states.*[31]

Religion again is not the bond which unites the members of a modern state: 'this identity too is something which modern states have found that they can do without.'³²

Hegel also denies that the state depended on there being uniform laws in all its provinces, or a uniform administration: 'All these things are only relatively important for the state, and for its true essence the form of their organization is immaterial.'³³

Again inequality of wealth, and hence of the tax burden between different classes are all irrelevant to the idea of the state.

Hegel is also clear that the state is not to be confused with civil society.³⁴ This is because if its specific end is laid down as the security and protection of property and personal freedom, then the interest of individuals as such becomes the ultimate end of the association, and it follows that membership of the state is something optional. Similarly the state cannot be considered a contract, because a contract is something based on arbitrary wills, opinion and capriciously given consent.

If the state is none of these things, what is it?

It is, says Hegel, 'mind objectified' and 'it is only as one of its numbers that the individual himself has objectivity, genuine individuality, and an ethical life.'³⁵

What does he mean by this?

### Notes

1 See Adam Ferguson, *An Essay on the History of Civil Society*, 1767 (Edinburgh), German trans. *Versuch über die Geschichte der bürgerlichen Gesellschaft*, 1768 (Rosenzweig as quoted in *Phil of Right*, p. x) for meaning of expression.
2 *Phil of Right*, para 199.
3 Ibid., para 238.
4 Ibid., para 200R.
5 Ibid., p. 10 (preface).
6 Ibid., para 206R.
7 See Ibid., para 184A: 'it might seem that universal ends would be more readily attainable if the universal absorbed the strength of the particular in the way described, for instance, in Plato's

Republic. But this . . . is only an illusion, since both universal and particular turn into one another and exist only for and by means of one another. If I further my ends, I further the ends of the universe, and this in turn furthers my end.'
8 Ibid., para 209.
9 Ibid., para 219.
10 Aridity of economic theories of politics.
11 *Phil of Right*, para 219R.
12 Ibid., para 195A.
13 Ibid., para 195.
14 Ibid., para 201.
15 Ibid., para 206.
16 Ibid., para 201A.
17 Ibid., para 243.
18 Ibid., para 244.
19 Ibid., para 244A.
20 Ibid., para 236R.
21 Ibid., para 241.
22 Ibid., para 244.
23 Explored in modern fiction, e.g. F. Scott Fitzgerald, *The Great Gatsby* (1926).
24 *Phil of Right*, para 252.
25 See Ibid., para 255R: no longer 'unorganized atoms of civil society'.
26 Ibid., para 253R.
27 Ibid., para 256.
28 Ibid., para 257.
29 Ibid., para 257R.
30 *Sittlich* is 'ethical' and *Sitten* are 'customs': 'Customs are ethical in the sense that they embody the rationality of those whose customs they are.' Knox in *Phil of Right*, para 350, f. 14. Ethical life is 'the good become alive' 142 the good is not merely something transcendent, it is substance risen to self-consciousness in individuals, Knox in *Phil of Right*, para 346 f. 1.
31 *Hegel's Political Writings*, trans. T. M. Knox, ed. Z. A. Pelczynski (Oxford, Oxford University Press, 1964), p. 158.
32 Ibid., pp. 158–9.
33 Ibid.
34 *Phil of Right*, para 258R.
35 Ibid.

# 12

# THE STATE

Perhaps we should here attend to a point which Hegel emphasizes more than once in the course of his argument about the state.

To say that the state is something different from a family or from a civil society, to say that it is not a contract the purpose of which is to protect the interest of particular individuals, is *not* to say that a state to be a state has to abolish, to cancel, or to inhibit the family, the civil society or the interests of particular individuals. On the contrary, the modern state, argues Hegel, would be impossible without family and civil institutions, and its great strength (and Hegel believed that the modern state is a much tougher structure than the ancient or the medieval) lies precisely in the conviction of its members – a conviction which becomes habitual and a ground for their behaviour as citizens – that their particular interests and satisfactions (in all their infinite variety) would be at risk but for the state – the state which is not an alien institution imposed from above, but rather is flesh of the citizens' own flesh. In other words, for Hegel, the state is no more and no less than the totality of the citizens – acting not as members of a family, or of a civil society, but as citizens.

Hegel has recourse to an analogy to clarify this complicated point. In a sentient being there is, in the first place, 'the dull movement which goes on internally, reproduction, internal self-nutrition, growth and digestion'.[1] In the second place, there is 'sensation moving outwards' or what Hegel calls 'irritability'. Both of these imply the existence of 'the nervous system as a whole, something inwardly organized; but this lives only in so far as [internal sensation and sensation moving outwards] are developed within it'. *Similarly*, the family and civil society are ethical institutions (ethical in the sense of the word I explained in my last lecture), 'institutions of the rational order which glimmers through them'. But for them the rational ethical order would not be seen to exist, but their ground, that which gives them meaning, significance, is not to be found in the institutions themselves. Hegel develops further the idea that there is a vital interconnection between the modern state on the one hand, and the family and civil society on the other.

> The concrete state is the whole, articulated into its particular groups. The member of a state is a member of such a group . . . and it is only as characterized in this objective way that he comes under consideration when we are dealing with the state.[2]

An individual is consciousness, mind, will. But an individual as mere consciousness is empty. Consciousness and will 'lose their emptiness and acquire a content and a living actuality only when they are filled with particularity, and particularity means determinacy . . . the single person attains his actual and living destiny for universality only when he becomes a member of a Corporation, a society etc.'

And in the modern state, for the citizen, politics, that is, that which concerns the state, is articulated through the communities, associations and corporations, to which he belongs.[3] And these associations, corporations, etc. find in the state the means of maintaining their particular ends. 'This', Hegel observes, 'is the secret of the patriotism of the citizens in the sense that they know the state as their substance, because it is the state that maintains their particular spheres of interest together with the title, authority, and welfare of these. In the corporation mind the rooting of the particular in the universal is directly entailed, and for this reason it is in that mind that the depth and strength which the state possesses in sentiment is seated.'[4]

'The political sentiment, patriotism pure and simple' is, Hegel tells us, *'a volition which has become habitual'*:

> This sentiment is, in general, *trust* . . . or the consciousness that my interest . . . is contained and preserved in another's (i.e. in the state's) interest and end.
> . . . In this way, this very other is immediately not an other in my eyes, *and in being conscious of this fact, I am free.*[5]

All this is to say how profoundly Hegel disagrees with Rousseau's stark contrast between the general will and the will of all, and his belief that partial associations are injurious to the state and subvert the citizens' proper loyalty to it, and how Hegel would have dismissed as pernicious fancy St Just's assertion that patriotism 'is so exclusive as to sacrifice everything to the public interest, without pity, without fear, without respect for humanity' and his other assertion that 'what produces the general good is always terrible.'[6]

The state, then, is its citizens. What are these citizens in the modern world? Members of families to be sure, who in adulthood are torn away from the protection of the family, and have to find their place in civil society. They are also individuals with their own tastes and inclinations who know, who have learnt, that they have a right to these tastes and inclinations. They are aware of themselves as subjectivities who not only have a right to their satisfactions, but also as subjectivities which are possessed of a conscience by which they are able to judge of the rightness and wrongness of actions, and this conscience is the court of last resort. They are all these things, and they are not solitaries – and it is because they are all these things that freedom for them cannot be the family, or the market, but only the state.

> The essence of the modern state is that the universal be bound up with the complete freedom of its particular members, and with *private well-being*.[7]...
>
> In the states of antiquity, the subjective end simply coincided with the state's will. In modern times, however, we make claims for private judgement, private willing, and private conscience.... *The determinations of the individual will are given an objective embodiment through the state and thereby they attain their truth and their actualization for the first time. The state is the one and only prerequisite of the attainment of particular ends and welfare.*[8]

In the state 'the universal does not prevail or achieve completion *except along with particular interests and through the co-operation of particular* knowing and willing.... The principle of modern states has *prodigious strength and depth because it allows the principle of subjectivity to progress to its culmination in the extreme of self-subsistent* personal particularity, and yet at the same time brings it to the substantive unity' of the state.[9]

It is not true, Hegel declares, that it is force which holds the state together. In fact 'its only bond is the fundamental sense of order'[10] in which differences hold themselves in unity, in which '*the interest of the whole is realized in and through particular ends.*'[11]

'The state . . . is both the law permeating all relationships within the state and also at the same time the manners and consciousness of its citizens.'[12] The state being both law and a manner of behaving, it becomes meaningless to ask who is to frame the constitution.[13] There must be a general congruence between law and the manners of those whose conduct is regulated by law. Therefore 'the constitution should not be regarded as something made, even though it has come into being in time. It must be treated rather as something *simply existent in and by itself*, [substance] as divine therefore, and constant, and so as exalted above the sphere of things that are made.'

The term 'divine' may surprise us, but in order to make sense of it we have to bear in mind the context of Hegel's thought on politics. It is with this context in mind that we should approach certain other statements of Hegel's which have been considered extravagant, scandalous, not to say sinister. In an addition to paragraph 258 we read (in Knox's translation) that the state is 'the march of God in the world', that the state is 'an actual God'. Again in the addition[14] to paragraph 272 we read that man must 'venerate the state as a secular deity'. About this language two things have to be said, that the associations or reverberations of certain words which Knox uses get in the way of our appreciating Hegel's meaning. For example, in the section on morality in *The Philosophy of Right* there is a subsection entitled 'Intention and Welfare'. The word 'welfare' in English – in Britain at any rate – has associations relating to expenditure by the government of monies gathered from taxpayers on (usually free) medical and social services available to the population. This particular association which the word has come to have seriously gets in the way of our following Hegel's argument, which is in fact about the well-being of the agent, and the relation between intentions to seek satisfactions and the actual achievement of well-being. Similarly, when we read that the state is the march of God in the world, the word 'march' conjures up for us images of a juggernaut mercilessly trampling on men in a bloody and irresistible progress, the more so that the work is a German work, declared by eminent writers to be the bible of German (or Prussian) militarism. The word for 'march' which Hegel uses is *Gang*; it has none of these connotations and means more 'course' or 'passage' than 'march'. Again 'actual God' may be misleading since the word 'actual' may seem to be used in order to lend emphasis to the assertion that the state is indeed God. But the word 'actual' is the translation of the word *wirklich* and the expression 'actual God' is in Hegel's original text *wirklicher Gott*. And by *wirklich* – which is a technical term in Hegel's vocabulary – we are to understand the synthesis of essence and existence. As we have seen earlier in this course of lectures, Hegel's religion can loosely be described as some kind of pantheism – we may add 'a dynamic pantheism' whereby the course of human history is God manifesting himself – hence his famous and equally scandalous statement (which occurs in the preface to *The Philosophy of Right*) that 'What is rational is actual and what is actual is rational.' In all these descriptions of the state, then, what Hegel means to emphasize is that the state is a human artifact which is also divine – divine because it is the means through which man can heal the rift within himself, feel utterly at home in the world, reconcile desirable differences with the unity without which difference is self-stultifying and destructive.

This is all I want to say in this course about Hegel's political thought. I will remind you that what I have said I meant to say in the context of these lectures, which are about 'the political thought of Hegel and Marx'. As you have seen not only does Hegel have a great deal to say about politics in the modern state, but also his reflection on politics is a properly philosophical one, taking its due place in a scheme where the religious, social and economic aspects of life have been considered and properly demarcated. We can say that Hegel properly speaking has a fully considered theory of politics which he has taken the trouble to work out in great detail. This is in great contrast to his followers and those who worked out their philosophical positions in the shadow of or in reaction to (and the two things do not necessarily rule out one another) Hegel's thought. What these followers and continuators were interested in mostly was the logic, the philosophy of history and, supremely, the philosophy of religion. This is true of Marx as well. Marx of course had a great deal to say about politics throughout his career, but the fact remains that he did not work out a theory of politics in the way in which Hegel worked it out in *The Philosophy of Right* or as Marx himself worked out a theory of economics in *Capital* and other writings.

When Hegel died in 1831 his philosophy was the dominant one in German universities. Dominant in the sense that he had a great number of disciples who carried on and developed what they took to be his teaching. But dominant also in the perhaps more important sense that his way of defining philosophical problems, and tackling them, was implicitly accepted. His philosophy and its vocabulary, in other words, constituted the accepted universe of discourse for philosophers but also for theologians. Hegel, as we have seen, began his career as a philosopher with a preoccupation with issues of Christian theology, and, as we have also seen, it was in wrestling with Christianity and its difficulties that he worked out an individual and original philosophical position. We can even go so far as to say that it is quite impossible to understand the character and thrust of Hegel's thought unless we are aware of its original and earliest preoccupations. The mature Hegel, as he worked out a logic, a philosophy of history, an aesthetic and a political philosophy, also worked out a philosophy of religion. In this philosophy of religion, the traditional dogmas of Christianity, the Incarnation, the Trinity, etc., were made to take their place in a philosophical scheme in which their significance was by no means what it had been in traditional teaching. To this enterprise of Hegel's there could be two opposite reactions. You could say that Hegel's philosophy of religion saved Christianity from bankruptcy, by disclosing the hidden philosophical significance of the Christian creeds, a significance independent of dubious historical proofs, and such as to establish Christianity as the last and highest religion, as indeed the truth of all the religions which have appeared in history. Or you could say that Hegel's philosophy of religion was in the last analysis profoundly subversive of Christianity. If you accepted this view, you could in turn adopt one of two attitudes. The first, which was highly exceptional, was to reject Hegel root and branch in the belief that the true God was the God of Abraham, Isaac and Jacob, and that the God of the philosophers, and Hegel's God in particular was a stumbling block, a snare and a delusion. This was the reaction of the Danish thinker Søren Kierkegaard (1813–55) who attacked Hegel's philosophy of religion as a pantheistic falsification of Christianity, and to the Hegelian dialectics in which he had been reared opposed a powerful existential dialectic of man existing in solitude before God, racked with sin, and seeking redemption through faith. Kierkegaard wrote in Danish, and it was only much later that his voice began to be heard at all. The second attitude which followed from the view that Hegel subverted Christianity was to applaud the enterprise as a necessary one, and to take the line that Hegel did not go far enough, that his method constituted a powerful weapon to use in the necessary demolition of Christianity – which was nothing but an obstacle to the liberation of humanity. These two interpretations of Hegel's philosophy of religion divided his disciples into the Right Hegelians and the Left Hegelians. The rift between them to start with was not political but theological. Indeed to judge by the writings of the people concerned, politics did not interest them particularly. Who were the people concerned? To take the most important among the Left Hegelians, David Strauss (1808–74), author of a famous *Life of Jesus* (translated by George Eliot) in which he tried to show that Christianity was based on a myth which developed between the death of Jesus and the writing of the Gospels in the second century of the Christian era. There was again Bruno Bauer (1809–82), Marx's friend of the Berlin years, who started out by being a Hegelian of the Right, but who then went beyond Strauss in his critique of the Christian Gospels, each one of which was invented by its author. Finally, and most important in our context, there was Ludwig Feuerbach (1804–72), the author of *The Essence of Christianity* (also translated by George Eliot), of the *Provisional Theses for the Reform of Philosophy* and of the *Principles of the Philosophy of the Future* which had such a great influence on Marx (and on Engels), and through which we may say that Hegelian thought was largely mediated to Marx.[15]

### Notes

1 *Phil of Right*, para 263A.
2 Ibid., para 308R.

3 Ibid., para 308.
4 Ibid., para 289R.
5 Ibid., para 286.
6 Quoted in E. Kedourie, *Nationalism*, 3rd edn. (London, Hutchinson, 1966), p. 18.
7 *Phil of Right*, para 260A.
8 Ibid., para 261A. See also Ibid., para 265A: 'The state is actual only when its members have a feeling of their own self-hood and it is stable only when public and private ends are identical. It has often been said that the end of the state is the happiness of the citizens. That is perfectly true. If all is not well with them, if their subjective aims are not satisfied, if they do not find that the state as such is the means to their satisfaction *then the footing of the state itself is insecure.*'
9 Ibid., para 260.
10 Ibid., para 268A.
11 Ibid., para 270A.
12 Ibid., para 274.
13 Ibid., para 273R.
14 Additions are culled from students' notes.
15 Marx, *Theses on Feuerbach*, 1845, and *Ludwig Feuerbach and the End of Classical German Philosophy*, 1888.

# 13

# FEUERBACH AND HEGEL

Like the young Hegel, Feuerbach began his philosophical career by being a student of theology. Born in 1804, he enrolled in the faculty of theology at Heidelberg in 1823. But the teaching in Heidelberg did not satisfy him, and after a year he obtained his father's consent to transfer to Berlin where Hegel taught; he did not study, however, in the faculty of philosophy, but again in the faculty of theology. But it was really Hegel who attracted Feuerbach to Berlin, because again like the young Hegel he was finding theology and the traditional Christian tenets unsatisfactory and unacceptable. In 1846 Feuerbach in an autobiographical piece wrote:

> I went to Berlin to follow Hegel's lectures, but also at the same time the lectures of the most famous theologians there [Schleiermacher being the best known]. I entered the University of Berlin highly divided within myself, unhappy and undecided; I already felt in myself the conflict between philosophy and theology, the necessity of sacrificing philosophy to theology or theology to philosophy. I followed the lectures of Schleiermacher and Neander, but I was unable to persevere in this for more than a short while. The theological mishmash of freedom and dependence, reason and faith, was

completely repellent to my soul which aspired to truth, i.e. to unity, decisiveness and absoluteness. For two years I followed Hegel's lectures.[1]

But for financial reasons Feuerbach had to transfer to Erlangen, where he graduated in 1828 with a thesis entitled 'Of Reason, One, Universal, Infinite'. The thesis was very much that of a disciple of Hegel's. In it Feuerbach argued that reason is 'the activity of the universal, as that which comprehends nature and gives it significance and unites thinking and being'.[2] Reason is clearly above religion. Reason is the universal enabling man to break through the limitations of individuality, and thus to unite with other men, while Christianity is the 'religion of egoism and individuality'.[3] 'In thinking I am thus mankind, not the individual, but no one in particular.' Feuerbach sent a copy of his dissertation to his Master, Hegel, calling himself his 'direct disciple', and proclaiming the exclusive reign of reason to which Christianity is subordinate. 'Christianity', he wrote to Hegel, 'cannot be considered the perfect and absolute religion. This cannot be anything but the reign of the reality of the Idea and of actual Reason.'

In 1830 Feuerbach published anonymously his *Thoughts on Death and Immortality*, which was a continuation and a working out of the ideas sketched out in his dissertation and in which was included an appendix of satirical-theological epigrams 'in which he announced that religion was merely a kind of insurance company'.[4] The appendix in particular created great scandal and put paid to any hopes Feuerbach may have had of an academic career. In the body of the work itself Feuerbach denied the immortality of the individual soul. Man's only dwelling-place, he argued, was this earth, and the only immortality lay in the species in which a man's spirit and his achievement survived to be handed down to successive generations to form part of the culture of humanity. Feuerbach's *Thoughts on Death and Immortality* may thus be considered as one of the first acts in what Father de Lubac has called (in a book published in 1945) the drama of atheist humanism – a drama which was first played out on the European stage, but which now has for its theatre the whole world.

It was with the publication in 1841 of *The Essence of Christianity*[5] that Feuerbach came to be widely known. Not only widely known, but also to be regarded as the most outstanding and most influential of the Left Hegelians. Just as *Thoughts on Death and Immortality* was a working out and amplification of Feuerbach's thesis, so *The Essence of Christianity* is the working out and amplification of the Hegelian ideas so daringly formulated in *Thoughts on Death and Immortality*. What Feuerbach wishes to establish in *The Essence of Christianity* may be quickly gathered from its table of contents. The work – following two introductory chapters – is divided into two parts: Part I, 'The True or Anthropological Essence of Religion', and Part II, 'The False or Theological Essence of Religion'. Feuerbach aims to uncover true religion so long hidden and disguised by theology, thereby liberating man from the shackles of false religion, and by liberating him to make it possible for him to accomplish the great things which humanity can accomplish. This was how Feuerbach put it in a set of public lectures which the German revolution of 1848–9 enabled him to give at Heidelberg. In these lectures on *The Essence of Religion*[6] Feuerbach declared that his whole purpose 'was to re-unite man with his spirit, to change "the friends of God into friends of man, believers into thinkers, worshippers into labourers, candidates for the next world into scholars of this world, Christians – who admit to being 'half-animal and half-angel' into men, complete men"'.

What is the essence of man which theology has denatured? What then is man? Man is distinguished from other animals because he has, and they do not have, religion: 'It is true that the old uncritical writers on natural history attributed to the elephant, among other laudable qualities, the virtue of religiousness, but the religion of elephants belongs to the realm of fable.' But the presence of religion in man in turn rests on an *essential* difference between him and the animals. This essential difference is consciousness but, Feuerbach is careful to add, 'consciousness *in the strict sense*'; 'for the consciousness implied in the feeling of self as an individual, in discrimination by the senses, in the perception and even judgement of outward things according to definite sensible signs, cannot be denied to brutes'.[7] *But* 'Consciousness in the strict sense is present only in a being to whom *his species, his essential nature is an object of thought*. The brute is indeed conscious of himself as an individual . . . but not as a species: hence he is without that consciousness which in its nature, as in its name, is akin to science. Where there is this higher consciousness there is a capability of science. Science is the cognizance of species. . . . only a being to whom his own species, his own nature, is an object of thought, can make the essential nature of other things or beings an object of thought.'

Man is a species being. As we shall see, this key idea of Feuerbach's was to become a key idea of Marx's. The idea of the species as the fulfilment of the individual had also occurred to D. F. Strauss who in the conclusion of his *Life of Jesus* (1835–6) had written 'It is not the way in which the idea realises itself to pour out its whole fullness in one example . . . rather it likes to spread out its riches in the multiplicity of examples which mutually complete themselves.' And again 'When thought of as belonging to an individual, a God-man, the qualities and function that the teaching of the Church attributes to Christ are contradictory, but in the species they live in harmony. Humanity is the unity of both natures, *finite spirit remembering its infinity*.'[8] Since the God-man is an absurdity and Jesus a myth, some such idea as species and species-being had to be the substitute – for they (the Left Hegelians) all felt that there had to be a substitute. There is no doubt that it was Feuerbach who articulated and developed the implications of this substitution of man for God. And this not only in *The Essence of Christianity*, but in other writings as well, of which the most important is the *Principles of the Philosophy of the Future* which he published in 1843. Let us consider these implications:

> *Man is divine*: If . . . feeling is the essential organ of religion, the nature of God is nothing else than an expression of the nature of feeling. The *true but latent sense* of the phrase 'Feeling is the organ of the divine', is, feeling is *the noblest, the most excellent*, i.e., the divine, in man. How couldst thou perceive the divine by feeling, if feeling were not in itself divine in its nature? The divine assuredly is known only by means of the divine – *God is known only by himself*. The divine nature which is discerned by feeling is in truth nothing else than feeling enraptured, in ecstasy with itself – feeling intoxicated with joy, blissful in its own plenitude.[9]
>
> *God possesses divine qualities because divine not vice-versa*: The Homeric gods eat and drink; – that implies eating and drinking is a divine pleasure. Physical strength is an attribute of the Homeric gods: Zeus is the strongest of the gods. Why? Because physical strength, in and by itself, was regarded as something glorious, divine. To the ancient Germans the highest virtues were those of the warrior; *therefore* their supreme god was the god of war, Odin. . . . *Not the attribute of the divinity, but the divineness or deity of the*

*attribute, is the first true Divine Being.* Thus what theology and philosophy have held to be God, the Absolute, the Infinite is not God; but that which they have held not to be God is God: namely the attribute, the quality, whatever has reality. . . . *The fact is not that a quality is divine because God has it,* but that God has it, because it is in itself divine.[10]

Or as Feuerbach strikingly puts it in the first of the *Provisional Theses for the Reform of Philosophy* which he published in 1842: *The secret of theology is anthropology.* And the secret which Feuerbach unveils for us is that man has dispossessed himself of all his most precious attributes and bestowed it on God: 'To enrich God, man must become poor; that God may be all man must be nothing.'[11]

But the truth is that God 'is an object of no being other than man, that he is a specifically human object, a secret of man. But, if God is only an object of man, what is revealed to us in his essence? Nothing but the essence of man. That whose object is the highest being is itself the highest being.'[12] For consider: St Thomas Aquinas said 'God is therefore the all-knowing because he knows the most particular things.' Feuerbach continues 'But this divine knowledge, which is only an imaginary conception and a fantasy in theology, became rational and real knowledge in the knowledge of the natural sciences gained through the telescope and microscope. . . . We have here an apparent example of the truth that man's conception of God is the human individual's conception of his own species, that God as the total of all realities or perfections is nothing other than the total attributes of the species . . . what the individual man does not know and cannot do all of mankind together knows and can do. Thus the divine knowledge that knows simultaneously every particular has its reality in the knowledge of the species.'[13] Therefore 'The single man for himself possesses the essence of man neither in himself as a moral being nor in himself as a thinking being. The essence of man is contained only in the community and unity of man with man; it is a unity, however, which rests only on the reality of the distinction between I and thou.' And 'Solitude is finiteness and limitation; community is freedom and infinity. Man for himself is man (in the ordinary sense); man with man – the unity of I and thou – is God.'[14]

'Two beings and their being distinguished from one another, this is the origin of religion – the Thou is the God of the I, because without you, I do not exist; the I depends on the Thou; without the Thou no I.'[15] 'Feuerbach', he says of himself, 'is a communal man, *communiste*.'[16]

Feuerbach, in the preface to his collected works 1846, wrote:

> It is a question to-day, you say, no longer of the existence or the non-existence of God, but of the existence or non-existence of man; not whether God is a creature whose nature is the same as ours but whether we human beings are to be equal among ourselves; not whether and how we can partake of the body of the Lord by eating bread but whether we have enough bread for our own bodies; not whether we render unto God what is God's and unto Caesar what is Caesar's, but whether we finally render unto man what is man's; not whether we are Christians or heathens, theists or atheists, but whether we are or can become men, healthy in soul and body, free, active and full of vitality. . . . The question concerning the existence or non-existence of God is for me nothing but the question concerning the existence or non-existence of man.[17]

Feuerbach's teaching created a great stir among the Young Hegelians, indeed among all those young men in Germany and elsewhere who felt discontented with things as they were, with the dead hand of obscurantist dogma and oppressive government. Richard Wagner, a refugee at Zurich after having taken part in the revolution at Dresden together with Bakunin in 1849, was given a copy of Feuerbach's *Thoughts on Death and Immortality*, and, as he records in his autobiography, he found the frankness with which Feuerbach dared to approach these issues highly interesting and very pleasing: 'It seemed to me glorious to know that the only true immortality was that which belonged to the sublime action and to the spiritual work of art.'[18] A Russian radical wrote to a fellow radical about 1847: 'All German idealism of the nineteenth century... drives only towards anthropotheism, to the point where, having reached its summit in the person of its latest standard-bearer and leading figure, Feuerbach, it calls things by their right name and exclaims with him *Homo homini deus est* – man is God unto man.'[19] And again that anthropotheism 'at least in its consummate form, as it is found in Feuerbach . . . pulls the whole man, without residue, into God. This is the second assumption of the God-Man, or the Man-God, who, according to legend, takes his body with him to heaven.' Or consider Bruno Bauer's view in a work of 1843, *Christianity Uncovered*. This book was immediately banned by the authorities of Zurich where it was published, and only a few copies survived in secret, until it was given to the world in 1927. In a chapter entitled 'Auto-divinisation'[20] Bauer says that it is 'modern criticism which has brought man to himself, which has allowed him to know himself. It has released men from their illusions and has taught them that self-consciousness is the only creative power in the world, more, that it is the world itself.'

Engels, writing in 1886, that is, some 45 years after the appearance of the *Essence of Christianity* (and no doubt attributing to Feuerbach some of his own later philosophical positions) is still vividly impressed with the impact of the work. 'One must oneself have experienced the liberating effect of this book to get an idea of it. Enthusiasm was general; we all became at once Feuerbachians.' Marx himself was also greatly impressed by the arguments of the *Essence of Christianity*, the *Provisional Theses* and the *Philosophy of the Future*. Consider for instance the article entitled 'Critique of Hegel's Philosophy of Right. Introduction' written in 1843–4 and published in the *German-French Annals*. The whole article bears the impress of Feuerbach's ideas, for example this characteristic passage:

> To be radical is to grasp things by the root. But for man the root is man himself. Clear proof of the radicalism of German Theory and its practical energy is the fact that it takes as its point of departure a decisive and *positive* transcendence of religion. The criticism of religion ends with the doctrine that for man the supreme being is man, and thus with the *categorical imperative* to overthrow all conditions in which man is a debased, enslaved, neglected and contemptible being.[21]

Marx's words show that for him Feuerbach's significance went far beyond the criticism of religion, that the truth that 'for man the supreme being is man' had radical consequences in society and politics. He was not the only one of whom this was true. Moses Hess (1812–75) wrote an article on 'The Essence of Money', also in 1843–4 and also published in the *German-French Annals*. Hess clearly draws on Feuerbach's teaching about religion and extends its application to economic life. Just as God has alienated for himself the human essence to the detriment of man, in the same way money has alienated the human essence also to the detriment of man. It is this alienation which sets man against man, and creates competition in which the concept of humanity is lost. So that a power which issues from man and his activity, which is the fruit of his work, comes to dominate him. Money dominates those who have it as well as those who do not have it.

> What God is for theoretical life, money is for the practical life of a world which is turned upside down: the alienated essence of men, their activity put on sale. Money is human value expressed in figures, it is the seal of our slavery, the indelible stigma of our servitude.[22]

It is the same order of ideas which Marx was to develop in *Capital*, notably in the celebrated chapter entitled 'The Mystery of the Fetishistic Character of Commodities':

> We are concerned only with a definite social relation between human beings, which, in their eyes, has here assumed the semblance of a relation between things. To find an analogy, *we must enter the nebulous world of religion*. In that world, the products of the human mind become independent shapes, endowed with lives of their own, and able to enter into relations with men and women. The products of the human hand do the same thing in the world of commodities. I speak of this as the *fetishistic character* which attaches to the products of labour, so soon as they are produced in the form of commodities.

Feuerbach, as I have said, was a Hegelian, and it is out of Hegelianism that he developed his ideas on religion. In fact had Feuerbach but known it, his ideas on theology and religion were remarkably like those of the young Hegel at the Tübinger Stift and in his Berne period. And as we have seen earlier in these lectures, it was because he found his own position ultimately unsatisfactory that Hegel was led to work out a philosophical position for himself which would be at once transparent, comprehensive and non-paradoxical. Feuerbach proved incapable of this, and his early philosophical impulse was to end in a crude and naive naturalism which may be summed up without injustice in the sentence which occurs in a book review which he wrote many years later: 'Man is what he eats.'

Feuerbach readily acknowledged himself Hegel's disciple. He wrote in 1840:

> Indeed, I stand in an intimate and influential relationship to Hegel . . . for I know him personally. . . . It was under his influence that I came to self-consciousness and world-consciousness. It was he who was my second father, as Berlin became my spiritual birthplace . . . Hegel was my teacher, I his student: I do not lie when I say that I acknowledge this fact today with thanks and joy.[23]

Feuerbach wrote these words a year or so following the publication of an article of his in the organ of the Left Hegelians, the *Halle Annals*, entitled 'Contribution to the Critique of Hegel's Philosophy'. In this long article Feuerbach accused the Hegelian philosophy of the same misdeeds which religion had perpetrated.[24] 'Hegel's system', he wrote, 'is the absolute self-alienation of reason.' His meaning is clarified for us by a few short sentences in the *Provisional Theses* of 1842:

> The essence of theology is the (*transcendent*) essence of man projected outside man: the essence of Hegel's logic is *transcendent* thought, man's thought put outside man.[25]
>
> In the same way as theology begins by dividing and alienating man in order subsequently to reidentify with him his alienated essence, similarly Hegel begins by fragmenting and dispersing the simple self-identical essence of nature and of man, in order forcibly to reunite what he had forcibly drawn apart.[26]

To abstract is to put the essence of nature *outside nature*, the essence of man *outside man*, the essence of thought *outside the act of thinking*. In basing his entire system on these acts of abstraction, Hegel's philosophy has alienated *man from himself*.[27]

Ideas, Feuerbach is saying, alienate man from his essence. What Hegel has done is to abstract ideas from the act of thinking and make them independent of man, make them stand over against man, controlling and dominating him in the same way as God is made in theology to be an independent being who controls and dominates man – who has actually created him.

For, says Feuerbach, 'I owe my existence never to the linguistic or logical bread – bread in itself – but always only to *this* bread, to the "unutterable"! Being that is founded on many such unutterable things is therefore itself something unutterable. It is indeed the ineffable. *Where words cease, life first begins.*'[28]

'The idea proves its worth through sensation.' But paradoxically 'sensation is made only into an attribute of the idea.' To save ourselves from this paradox we must make 'the sensuous into its own subject and give it an absolutely independent, divine, and primary meaning which is not first derived from the idea'.[29]

Marx was enormously impressed by this criticism of Hegel. Feuerbach, he says in *The Economic and Philosophical Manuscripts* (1844), is 'the only person who has a *serious* and a *critical* attitude to the Hegelian dialectic and who has made real discoveries in this field. He is the true conqueror of the old philosophy.'

> Feuerbach's great achievement is: (1) To have shown that philosophy is nothing more than religion brought into thought and developed in thought, and that it is equally to be condemned as another form and mode of existence of the estrangement of man's nature. (2) To have

founded *true materialism* and *real science* by making the social relation of 'man to man' the basic principle of his theory.[30]

Hegelian mystification consists in setting up imaginary entities and taking them for reality:

> my true religious existence is my existence in the *philosophy of religion*, my true political existence is my existence in the *philosophy of right*, my true natural existence is my existence in the *philosophy of nature*, my true artistic existence is my existence in the *philosophy of art* and my true *human* existence is my existence in *philosophy*.[31]

### Notes

1 Eugene Kamenka, *The Philosophy of Ludwig Feuerbach* (London, Routledge & Kegan Paul, 1970), p. 23. Henri Arvon, *Ludwig Feuerbach ou la transformation du sacré* (Paris, Presses Universitaires de France, 1957), p. 9.
2 Kamenka, pp. 23–4.
3 Arvon, p. 11.
4 Kamenka, p. 24.
5 Feuerbach, *The Essence of Christianity*, trans. Marion Evans [George Eliot, pseud.] (London, John Chapman, 1854).
6 See William J. Brazill, *The Young Hegelians* (New Haven and London, Yale University Press, 1970), pp. 152–3.
7 *Essence of Christianity*, pp. 1–2.
8 David McLellan, *The Young Hegelians and Karl Marx* (London, Macmillan, 1969) pp. 91–2.
9 *Essence of Christianity*, p. 9.
10 Ibid., p. 21.
11 Ibid., p. 26.
12 Feuerbach, *Principles of the Philosophy of the Future*, 1843, 89 (p. 10).
13 Ibid., 812 (16–17).
14 Ibid., 859 & 60 (p. 71).
15 Louis Althusser, trans. Ludwig Feuerbach – *Manifestes philosophiques* (Paris, Presses Universitaires de France, 1960), p. 304 Reply to Stirner 1845.
16 Ibid., 313.

17 Kamenka, p. 17.
18 Arvon, pp. 17–18 .
19 See Kamenka, p. 154 and p. 16.
20 See Arvon, pp. 81–2.
21 Marx, *Early Writings*, introduced by Lucio Colletti, trans. Rodney Livingstone and Gregor Benton (London, Penguin, 1975), p. 251.
22 Arvon, p. 110.
23 Brazill, p. 145.
24 *Manifestes*, p. 40.
25 Ibid., pp. 143–5, 813.
26 Ibid., p. 814.
27 Ibid., p. 820.
28 Feuerbach, *Philosophy of the Future*, 828 (43–4).
29 Ibid., 831 (50–1).
30 Marx, *Early Writings*, pp. 381–2.
31 Ibid., pp. 393–4.

# 14
# MARX AND HIS CRITICISM OF HEGEL

At the end of my last lecture I quoted a passage in which Marx accuses Hegel of mystification in setting up imaginary entities and taking them for reality. Sarcastically, he represents Hegel as believing that 'my true religious existence is my existence in the *philosophy of religion*, my true political existence is my existence in the *philosophy of right*, my true natural existence is my existence in the *philosophy of nature*, my true artistic existence is my existence in the *philosophy of art* and my true *human* existence is my existence in *philosophy*.' This passage appears in the so-called *Economic and Philosophical Manuscripts* which Marx wrote in Paris between April and August 1844. The *Manuscripts*, mostly devoted to economic questions in which Marx was beginning to be enormously interested, ends with a section – approximately a sixth of the whole work in length – in which Marx provides a *Critique of Hegel's Dialectic and General Philosophy*. The *Critique* concentrates on Hegel's *Phenomenology of Spirit* and particularly on its last chapter 'Absolute Knowledge'. Repetitive, compressed and obscure as this section of the *Manuscripts* is, yet it is of fundamental interest, particularly if we are examining the way in which Hegel's ideas were mediated to Marx, and if we are trying to compare the political thought of Hegel and Marx. There is only one other fairly substantial work by Marx – which he also left unpublished – which deals directly with Hegel's thought and specifically with his political thought, namely the *Critique of Hegel's Doctrine of the State*, which Marx wrote between March and August 1843, and which is a commentary on paragraphs 261–313 of *The Philosophy of Right*. To these two writings we may add one other short writing which Marx did publish, the article entitled 'A Contribution to the Critique of Hegel's Philosophy of Right. Introduction', which appeared in the first and only issue of the *German-French Yearbooks* in February 1844. These three writings are almost all we have to enable us to understand Marx's own view of Hegel's thought and how Marx formulated his own *specifically* political thinking and contrasted it with Hegel's. And we may here bear in mind a point which I made in the first lecture in this course, namely that one difficulty in studying the political thought of Hegel *and* Marx is that while Hegel wrote a great deal on politics and in particular a full-dress treatise on political philosophy, there is nothing of the kind in Marx's writings, and that we are for the most part reduced to making out what Marx thought about politics by extrapolating from his work on economics, and from occasional, if voluminous, journalistic and polemical writings. Marx himself, it is clear, intended to write a counterpart to Hegel's *Philosophy of Right*. The *Economic and Philosophical Manuscripts* begin with a preface which shows that Marx at one point at any rate intended these manuscripts to be the basis or the draft of a published work. In this preface Marx refers to his article in the *German-French Yearbooks* where he had announced a critique of the *Hegelian* philosophy of right. While preparing this for publication, I found that to combine criticism directed only against speculation with criticism of the various subjects themselves was quite unsuitable; it hampered the development of the argument and made it more difficult to follow. Moreover the wealth and diversity of the subjects to be dealt with would have fitted into a *single* work only if I had written in aphorisms, and an aphoristic presentation, for its part, would have given the impression of arbitrary systematization. I shall therefore publish the critique of law, morals, politics, etc., in a series of separate independent pamphlets and finally attempt, in a special work, to present them once again as a connected whole, to show the relationship between the parts and to try to provide a critique of the speculative treatment of the material. That is why the present work only touches on the interconnection of political economy and the state, law, morals, civil life, etc., in so far as political economy itself particularly touches on these subjects.[1]

This passage gives us, in the first place, an idea of Marx's ambitions as a thinker; we would not be exaggerating if we thought that Marx looked upon himself as another – and better – Hegel whose life's work would be characterized by the same all-embracing universality, but would be free from the mystification which infected Hegel's philosophy. We would also therefore not be mistaken in viewing Marx's writings on economics as the fragment or the torso of a much larger project which Marx was diverted from realizing. Diverted by his consuming interest in economic questions, by his political activities, by his journalism (by means of which he earned his living) and by his lengthy polemics with fellow Left Hegelians and, later on, with fellow socialists. The reason why, in a comparison between the political thought of Hegel and

Marx, the time devoted to Marx's ideas should be so much shorter than that devoted to Hegel's should now also become apparent. There is very much less to consider in Marx's case than in Hegel's, and what there is, is fragmentary and not fully thought out. But, more important, his philosophical strategy is such, we might conclude, that the political has a very subordinate and humble place in his system. It is 'superstructure'.

Be this as it may, there ought to be no doubt that Marx's writings of 1843–4 (which remained unknown during his lifetime and long afterwards – *The Critique of Hegel's Doctrine of the State* being published only in 1927, and the *Economic and Philosophical Manuscripts* only in 1932) are essential, in the same way as Hegel's early writings are, to understanding the mainsprings of his thought. For these early writings enable us to see what the questions were to which the *Capital*, the *Critique of Political Economy*, and *The Communist Manifesto* were the answer. It is essential to stress this because after the publication of Marx's early writings a controversy arose as to whether there were two Marxes, the earlier and the later, the 'humanistic' and the 'scientific'. This controversy has no substance, since (a) there is no incompatibility between the 'earlier Marx' and the 'later Marx', there is, rather, clear and undoubted continuity, and (b) Marx himself was not only aware of this continuity, but indicated quite clearly that his later work – *Capital* and the rest – arose out of his study of, and dissatisfaction with, Hegel.

Thus as late as 1873, that is ten years before his death, in the preface to the second German edition of *Capital*, Marx defined his relationship to Hegel:

> Nearly thirty years ago, I criticised the mystifying aspect of the Hegelian dialectic. But at the very time when I was working at the first volume of *Das Kapital* [which was

published in 1867], the peevish and arrogant mediocrities who nowadays have the ear of the educated public in Germany, were fond of treating Hegel . . . as a 'dead dog'. That was why I frankly proclaimed myself a disciple of that great thinker, and even, in *Das Kapital*, toyed with the use of Hegelian terminology when discussing the theory of value. Although in Hegel's hands dialectic underwent a mystification, this does not obviate the fact that he was the first to expound the general forms of its movement in a comprehensive and fully conscious way. In Hegel's writings dialectic stands on its head. You must turn it right way up again if you want to discover the rational kernel that is hidden away within the wrappings of mystification.[2]

Again in the preface to the *Critique of Political Economy*, which he published in 1859, Marx gives us some details of his intellectual history which indicate the crucial importance for his later work of his engagement with Hegel in 1843–4.[3] He tells us that his work as editor of the *Rheinische Zeitung* in 1842–3 led him to be interested in political economy and to entertain doubts about some French socialist theories which then held the stage:

> The first work which I undertook to dispel the doubts assailing me was a critical re-examination of the Hegelian philosophy of law. . . . My inquiry led me to the conclusion that neither legal relations nor political forms could be comprehended whether by themselves or as the basis of a so-called general development of the human mind, but that on the contrary they originate in the material conditions of life, the totality of which Hegel, following the example of English and French thinkers of the eighteenth century, embraces within the term 'civil society'. . . . The general conclusion at which I arrived and which, once reached, became the guiding principle of my studies can be summarised as follows. In the social production of their existence, men inevitably

enter into definite relations, which are independent of their will, namely relations of production appropriate to a given stage in the development of their material forces of production. The totality of these relations of production constitutes the economic structure of society, the real foundation, on which arises a political superstructure and to which correspond definite forms of social consciousness. *The mode of production of material life conditions the general process of social, political and intellectual life. It is not the consciousness of men that determines their existence, but their social existence that determines their consciousness.*

In the preface to the second German edition of *Capital* Marx makes this point in different terms, and these different terms are also worth attending to in our context here:

My own dialectical method is not only fundamentally different from the Hegelian dialectical method, but is its direct opposite. For Hegel, the thought process (which he actually transforms into an independent subject, giving to it the name 'idea') is the demiurge of the real; and for him the real is only the outward manifestation of the idea. *In my view, on the other hand, the ideal is nothing other than the material when it has been transposed and translated inside the human head.*[4]

A number of things may be said about these two passages from the *Critique of Political Economy* and *Capital* respectively: first, Marx's statements about his views on economy, society and politics originating in an engagement with Hegel are borne out by the evidence of his writings of 1843–4. Second, the ideas expressed in these two passages, for example, 'the ideal is nothing other than the material when it has been transposed and translated inside the human head' and 'it is not the consciousness of men that determines their existence, but their social existence that determines their consciousness', have now become so current and so accepted that they have ceased to puzzle, they have come to be taken for granted, to seem a truism which it is foolish and wrong-headed to question or dispute – this may be the result not only of the very wide currency which Marxism has gained as a result of the triumph of Bolshevism in Russia and elsewhere, but also because Marx's view appeals powerfully, and at the same time seems to give sanction to what is called the philosophy of 'common sense', that 'common sense' which holds that the tangible, the visible, etc., is in some sense more real than, superior to, that which cannot be touched by the hand or seen by the eyes.[5] The difficulties and ultimate untenability of such a view are of course well known to students of the history of philosophy, but these difficulties notwithstanding it requires a great effort not to believe in the legislative authority of the tangible and the visible. This leads me to the third comment on Marx's statements – which is that far from being the simple promptings of common sense these ideas are in reality part of a complex and abstruse argument in which Marx went badly astray – went astray, or rather was led astray by his mentor Feuerbach.

As we have seen from the last lecture, Feuerbach, in an article of 1839, in the *Provisional Theses for the Reform of Philosophy* of 1842 and in *The Principles of the Philosophy of the Future* of 1843, argued that just as theology invented a God who alienated man from his essence, so Hegel too by means of his philosophy alienated man from himself. This view, as I have said earlier, impressed Marx enormously. In the preface to the *Economic and Philosophical Manuscripts* Marx declared that 'It is only with Feuerbach that *positive* humanistic and naturalistic criticism begins . . . they are the only writings since Hegel's *Phenomenology* and *Logic* to contain a real theoretical revolution,'[6] and, in

# Marx and his Criticism of Hegel      173

the section on Hegel in the *Manuscripts*, that 'Feuerbach has destroyed the foundations of the old dialectic and philosophy,' that he is 'the only person who has a *serious* and a *critical* attitude to the Hegelian dialectic and who has made real discoveries in this field. He is the true conqueror of the old philosophy.'[7]

Marx's own criticism of Hegel is very much Feuerbach's, namely that Hegel has inverted the real order of things, and made that which man has produced by his own activity the real author of man and his world. According to Marx, Hegel somehow or another seeks to establish that the real existence belongs only to the categories of his Logic, that it is these categories which govern all human activity, that they are in some sense prior to man and superior to him, that Hegel, in other words, is like a crazy scientist who has invented and activated a robot and who comes to delude himself that the robot is his master.[8]

> The man estranged from himself is also the thinker estranged from his *essence*, i.e. from his natural and human essence. His thoughts are therefore fixed phantoms existing outside nature and man. In his *Logic* Hegel has locked up all these phantoms.[9]
>
> In Hegel, apart from or rather as a consequence of the inversion we have already described, this act appears to be merely formal because it is abstract and because it is seen only as *abstract thinking being*, as self-consciousness.[10]

This for Hegel is 'the final expression of human life' and 'this final expression' leads to the alienation of man's essence. For this process of 'abstract thinking' 'must have a bearer, a subject; but the subject comes into being only as the result; this result, the subject knowing itself as absolute self-consciousness, is therefore *God*, the self-knowing *and self-manifesting idea*. Real man and real nature become mere predicates, symbols of this hidden, unreal man and this unreal nature. Subject and predicate therefore stand in a relation of absolute inversion to one another; a *mystical subject-object* or *subjectivity encroaching upon the object*, the *absolute subject* as *a process*, as a *subject* which *alienates* itself and returns to itself from alienation . . . pure, *ceaseless* revolving within itself.'[11] What is the activity of this monstrous all devouring subject?

> The way in which consciousness is, and in which something is for it, is *knowing*. Knowing is its only act. Hence something comes to exist for consciousness in so far as it *knows* that *something*. Knowing is its only objective relationship. It knows the nullity of the object, i.e. that the object is not distinct from it . . . in that it knows the object as its own *self-alienation*; that is, it knows itself – i.e. it knows knowing considered as an object – in that the object is only the *appearance* of an object, an illusion, which in essence is nothing more than knowing itself which has confronted itself with itself and hence with a *nullity*, a something which has *no* objectivity outside knowing. Knowing knows that when it relates itself to an object it is only *outside* itself, alienates itself; that it only appears to itself as an object, or rather, that what appears to it as an object is only itself.[12]

This is why, Marx declares in the passage I have quoted at the beginning of this lecture, for Hegel 'my true religious existence is my existence in *the philosophy of religion*, my true political existence is my existence in *the philosophy of right*,' etc.[13]

But it is clear that Marx has gravely misunderstood Hegel. Hegel is not saying that all artistic activity is an illusion, the reality being the philosophy of fine art, all religious activity is an illusion, the reality being the philosophy of religion, all political activity an illusion, the reality being the philosophy of right. What all these philosophical investigations do, rather, is to uncover and articulate the respective principles of these activities. To take one example. In the preface to the *Philosophy of Right* Hegel says:

> After all, the truth about Right, Ethics and the state is as old as its public recognition and formulation in the law of the land, in the morality of everyday life, and in religion. What more does this truth require – since the thinking mind is not content to possess it in this ready fashion? It requires to be grasped in thought as well.[14]

This is exactly what is involved in the study of nature:

> So far as nature is concerned, people grant that it is nature as it is which philosophy has to bring within its ken, that the philosopher's stone lies concealed somewhere, somewhere within nature itself.[15]

Or consider an example which occurs in Marx's own argument. Marx does see that 'Hegel adopts the standpoint of modern political economy. He sees *labour* as the *essence*, the self-confirming essence, of man.'[16] So far so good, we might say, for this is an accurate account of Hegel, as anyone who has read Hegel on civil society, or on the master and the servant will recognize. But what follows is therefore all the more flabbergasting. For what does Marx tell us? He tells us that 'the only labour Hegel knows and recognizes is *abstract mental* labour'! This is no more than word-spinning, abstract mental labour with a vengeance. Hegel's thought is an attempt to grasp the concrete all at once in all its complex facets – its compulsion residing in the desire to describe how man can be free and at home in the world. We can now see the real ground – and we can also see how groundless it is – of Marx's statement in the preface to the second edition of *Capital* that for Hegel, the thought process (which he actually transforms into an independent subject, giving to it the name 'idea') is 'the demiurge of the real' and that 'for him the real is only the outward manifestation of the idea.'[17] We can also see the reason why in the preface to the *Critique of Political Economy* Marx sets up a contrast between 'existence' and 'consciousness' when he says that 'It is not the consciousness of men that determines their existence, but their social existence that determines their consciousness.' This sets up an opposition between 'consciousness' and 'existence' and gives 'existence' the priority. The true account, as Hegel saw, was a dialectical relation between the two. For Marx, however, 'consciousness' has come to stand for an object whose only attribute is knowledge, who spins concepts out of his mind, and who labours under the illusion that such concepts create and control reality. This was mystification, and a mystification which sooner or later proved itself bankrupt: 'the abstraction which comprehends itself as abstraction knows itself to be nothing; it must relinquish itself, the abstraction, and so arrives at something which is its exact opposite, *nature*. Hence the whole of the *Logic* is proof of the fact that abstract thought is nothing for itself and that only *nature* is something.'[18]

'For Hegel, human nature, man, is equivalent to *self-consciousness*.'[19] But for Feuerbach and Marx

> Man is directly a *natural being*. As a natural being and as a living natural being he is on the one hand equipped with *natural powers*, with *vital powers*, he is an *active* natural being. . . . On the other hand, as a natural, corporeal, sensuous, objective being he is a *suffering*, conditioned and limited being, like animals and plants. . . . To say that man is a *corporeal*, living, real, sensuous, objective being with natural powers means, that he has *real, sensuous objects* as the object of his being and of his vital expression, or that he can only *express* his life in real,

sensuous objects. . . . *Hunger* is a natural *need*; it therefore requires a *nature* and an *object* outside itself in order to satisfy and still itself. Hunger is the acknowledged need of my body for an *object* which exists outside itself and which is indispensable to its integration and to the expression of its essential nature. . . .

To be sensuous, i.e. to be real, is to be an object of sense, a *sensuous* object, and thus to have sensuous objects outside oneself, objects of one's sense perception.

But man is not only a natural being; he is a *human* natural being; i.e. he is a being for himself and hence a *species-being* . . . History is the true natural history of man.[20]

What the bearing of this doctrine is on economics, society and politics Marx works out elsewhere in the *Manuscripts* and in the *Critique of Hegel's Doctrine of the State.*

### Notes

1 Marx, *Early Writings*, pp. 280–1.
2 Marx, *Capital*, p. lix.
3 Marx, *Early Writings*, pp. 425–6.
4 *Capital*, p. lix.
5 Naive realism – the philosophy of the first blush.
6 Marx, *Early Writings*, p. 281.
7 Ibid., pp. 380–1.
8 The Cabinet not of Dr Caligari but of Prof Higgins.
9 Marx, *Early Writings*, p. 398.
10 Ibid., pp. 395–6.
11 Ibid., p. 396.
12 Ibid., p. 392.
13 Ibid., pp. 393–4.
14 *Phil of Right*, p. 3.
15 Ibid., p. 4.
16 Marx, *Early Writings*, p. 386.
17 To be – To be conscious of being – and mind mastering and embracing being and consciousness.
18 Marx, *Early Writings*, p. 397.
19 Ibid., p. 387.

20 Ibid., pp. 389–91. Hegel on hunger: not hunger but what one chooses to do about it.

# 15

# MARX ON HEGEL

As we saw when we examined Marx's arguments in the *Economic and Philosophical Manuscripts* of 1844, Marx criticized Hegel for failing to understand that 'abstract thought is nothing for itself and that only *nature* is something.'[1] This line of criticism is one to which Marx (and later on *Marxism* as well) faithfully adhered to. The classic expression of this criticism we may take to be Marx's statement in the preface to the *Critique of Political Economy* that 'It is not the consciousness of men that determines their existence, but their social existence that determines their consciousness.' The preface where this statement occurs is dated January 1859, but Marx had already arrived at this conclusion – never to move beyond it – some 15 years earlier, in the Paris *Manuscripts* of 1844, as well as in the commentary on paragraphs 261–313 of Hegel's *Philosophy of Right* which he wrote in 1843. This commentary is for us a valuable document, not only because it helps to clarify Marx's understanding of Hegel, which would have been extremely difficult if we had only the Paris *Manuscripts* of the following year, but also because the commentary (unlike the *Manuscripts*) is concerned with a writing of Hegel's where economic and political questions as such are methodically discussed – which of course is not the case with the *Logic* and the

*Phenomenology* with which Marx was preoccupied in the *Manuscripts*. The value of the *Manuscripts* lies in the fact that they try to bring out into the open the philosophical assumptions which underlie Marx's critique of Hegel's political thought.

Leaving aside for the moment these fundamental assumptions – and about their cogency one must, as I have said in my last lecture, entertain the gravest doubts – what in fact does Marx say about Hegel's views in the *Philosophy of Right*? As I have said, his manuscript is a commentary on paragraphs 261–313. These paragraphs are in subsection 3 of part III of the *Philosophy of Right*. Part III is devoted to the Ethical Life – in Hegel's sense of the term – and subsection 3 deals with the state and follows the discussion of the family and of civil society. We do not know why Marx chose to begin his commentary at this particular point of Hegel's treatise. As anyone familiar with the *Philosophy of Right* knows, Hegel's argument is fairly tightly knit, and constructed in such a way that the later sections depend heavily on what Hegel had tried to establish in the earlier sections. As readers of the work also know, these earlier sections (and in particular the short but very difficult introduction) are what one must come to grips with if one is to understand (let alone refute) Hegel's argument. Confining ourselves, however, to subsection 3 (on part of which Marx wrote his commentary), we know that Hegel tried to show the necessity of the state for securing and maintaining freedom as the modern world has come to understand it, by showing how the civil society and the family cannot possibly be autonomous self-subsistent institutions, by showing that their functioning leads to situations where they have to be transcended (*aufgehoben*), because such situations show up the limitations of the family and the market as human associations. Marx in no way attempts to come to grips with this fundamental point in this part of the *Philosophy of Right*. Rather, he relies – somewhat uncritically – on Feuerbach's contention that Hegel's philosophy is a mystified inversion of the real world, and on the related contention that 'nature' or 'existence' has primacy or priority – in some sense (and sometimes one has the impression that this is the fairly crude idea that what can be touched, seen, etc. is more 'real' than what can be thought) – over 'thought' or 'consciousness'. Marx accuses Hegel of 'logical, pantheistic mysticism'.[2] Why? Because in the real world 'the family and civil society are the preconditions of the state; they are the true agents.'[3] Again 'the family and civil society are real parts of the state, real spiritual manifestations of will, they are the state's forms of existence; the family and civil society make themselves into the state. They are the driving force.'[4] This Marx affirms rather than argues is the reality. What does Hegel say? 'According to Hegel, however, [the family and civil society] are *produced* by the real Idea; it is not the course of their own life that joins them together to comprise the state, but the life of the Idea which has distinguished them from itself.' These observations are by way of a commentary on Hegel's paragraph 262 which runs like this: 'The real Idea is mind, which, sundering itself into the two ideal spheres of its concept, family and civil society, enters upon its finite phase, but it does so only in order to rise above its ideality and become explicit as infinite real mind.' Now, if one takes this passage on its own, without regard to what Hegel means by Idea or mind, and without regard to the context in which this passage finds its place, then it is possible to give – or gain – the impression that Hegel is talking of a ghostly Idea which he believes to bring forth and to control in some mysterious way 'real' entities like family and civil society. But this is to misunderstand Hegel, and perhaps wilfully to misunderstand him. Because paragraph 262 comes after paragraph 261 in which Hegel says that 'the strength' of the modern state 'lies in the unity of its own universal end and aim with the particular interests of individuals'. Further, paragraph 261 (with which Marx's commentary begins though he does not comment on this passage) comes after paragraph 260 in which Hegel declares:

> The state is the actuality of concrete freedom. But concrete freedom consists in this, that personal individuality and its particular interests not only achieve their complete development and gain explicit recognition for their right (as they do in the sphere of the family and civil society) but, for one thing, they also pass over of their own accord into the interest of the universal, and, for another thing, they know and will the universal; they even recognize it as their own substantive mind; they take it as their end and aim and are active in its pursuit. The result is that the universal does not prevail or achieve completion except along with particular interests and through the co-operation of particular knowing and willing; and individuals likewise do not live as private persons for their own ends alone, but in the very act of willing these they will the universal in the light of the universal, and their activity is consciously aimed at none but the universal. The principle of modern states has prodigious strength and depth because it allows the principle of subjectivity to progress to its culmination in the extreme of self-subsistent personal particularity, and yet at the same time brings it back to substantive unity and so maintains this unity in the principle of subjectivity itself.

This paragraph should be enough (and if it were not, one could point, if necessary, to the 259 other paragraphs which precede and explain it) to show that for Hegel the Idea is not some mystificatory reification which he has allowed Frankenstein-like to terrorize and dominate the world of men. Rather for him the Idea is inseparable from the thoughts and actions of men which, as Hegel correctly observes, find satisfaction in aiming at the universal as well as at the particular, indeed cannot find satisfaction if they aim merely at the particular.

But having established to his satisfaction that the Idea is a ghost in the machine, that Hegel's world is an inverted world, Marx proceeds to put this inverted world right side up: 'Just as religion does not make man, but rather man makes religion, so the constitution does not make the people, but the people make the constitution.'[5] 'The state is an abstraction. Only the people is a concrete reality.'[6] Therefore 'Democracy is the solution to the *riddle* of every constitution.'[7]

But what does Marx mean by democracy? Marx makes a distinction between *form* and *content*. 'The *political* republic is democracy within the abstract form of the state.'[8] 'Property etc., in short the whole content of law and the state, is broadly the same in North America as in Prussia. Hence the *republic* in America is just as much a mere *form* of the state as the monarchy here. The content of the state lies beyond these constitutions.' It was in The German Ideology which Marx wrote together with Engels in 1845–6 and in The Communist Manifesto which they wrote in January 1848 that the well-known Marxist conclusions are drawn from this critique of the *Philosophy of Right*:

> The form of intercourse determined by the existing productive forces at all previous historical stages, and in its turn determining these, is *civil society*. . . . this civil society is the true source and theatre of all history, and [we see] how absurd is the conception of history held hitherto, which neglects the *real relationship* and

confines itself to high-sounding dramas of princes and states.

For Marx these 'real relationships' have a privileged status in history:

take the case of sugar and coffee which have proved their world-historical importance in the nineteenth century by the fact that the lack of these products, occasioned by the Napoleonic Continental system, caused the Germans to rise against Napoleon, and thus became the real basis of the glorious Wars of Liberation of 1813.[9]

The material life of individuals, . . . their mode of production and form of intercourse, which mutually determine each other – this is the real basis of the State and remains so at all stages at which division of labour and private property are still necessary. . . . These actual relations are in no way created by the State power; on the contrary they are the power creating it.[10] . . .

To this modern private property corresponds the modern State, which, purchased gradually by the owners of property by means of taxation, has fallen entirely into their hands through the national debt.[11] . . .

The State is the form in which the individuals of a ruling class assert their common interests.[12]

The executive of the modern state is but a committee for managing the common affairs of the bourgeoisie.[13]

But it is not a question only of the state being the expression of material interests in civil society:

The ruling ideas are nothing more than the ideal expression of the dominant material relationships, the dominant material relationships grasped as ideas. . . . The individuals composing the ruling class possess among other things consciousness, and therefore think. Insofar, therefore, as they rule as a class and determine the extent and compass of an epoch, it is self-evident that they do this in its whole range, hence among other things rule also as thinkers, as producers of ideas, and regulate the production and distribution of the ideas of their age: thus their ideas are the ruling ideas of the epoch. For instance, in an age and in a country where royal power, aristocracy and bourgeoisie are contending for mastery and where, therefore, mastery is shared, the doctrine of the separation of powers proves to be the dominant idea and is expressed as an 'eternal law'.[14]

In sum

This conception of history depends on our ability to expound the real process of production, starting out from the material production of life itself, and to comprehend the form of intercourse connected with this and created by this mode of production (i.e. civil society in its various stages) as the basis of all history; and to show it in its action as State, to explain all the different theoretical products and forms of consciousness, religion, philosophy, ethics, etc. etc. and trace their origins and growth from that basis.

This method

remains constantly on the real *ground* of history; it does not explain practice from the idea but explains the formation of ideas from material practice; and accordingly it comes to the conclusion that all forms and products of consciousness cannot be dissolved by mental criticism . . . but only by the practical overthrow of the actual social relations which gave rise to this idealistic humbug; that not criticism but revolution is the driving force of history, also of religion, of philosophy and all other types of theory.[15]

For Marx then, there can be, properly speaking, no political thought. It is something which can have no worth of its own, it is a mystificatory account, in the same way as religion is, of the relationships of production, of the condition of civil society. What then is the condition of civil society? Here too, we can say that Feuerbach constitutes the decisive influence on Marx's thought. Just as in religion, Christianity is the alienated essence of man, just as in philosophy the Idea or consciousness is alienated existence, so in civil society alienation now obtains. Alienation of labour into private property, an alienation with which the division of labour is somehow connected. It is this alienation which is the real secret of the existence of the state. 'Man's self-esteem,' wrote Marx to Ruge in May 1843, 'his sense of freedom must be reawakened. . . . This sense vanished from the world with the Greeks, and with Christianity it took up residence in the blue mists of heaven.'[16] When he wrote these words Marx had not yet worked out how exactly this freedom had disappeared and what must consequently be done to regain it. But by 1844–5, that is, from the time of the Paris *Manuscripts* and *The German Ideology* he came to have an explanation of this alienation and of its mechanism. In the spring and summer of 1844 Marx read and made excerpts from James Mill's *Elements of Political Economy* and added his own comments to them. It is here that we see him working out the crucial distinction between use-value and exchange-value which is one of the principal analytical weapons which he uses in *Capital*. Exchange requires a medium of exchange. But this mediating function again assumes a monstrous Frankenstein-like life. It becomes 'the property of a material thing external to man, viz. money. If a man himself alienates this mediating function [like Moses Hess] he becomes active only as a lost dehumanized creature.'[17] 'Hence this mediator is the lost estranged essence of private property . . . ; it is the alienated mediation of human production with human production, the alienated species-activity of man. . . . The mediating movement of man engaged in exchange is not a social, human movement, it is no human relationship.'[18]

In production for exchange man is estranged from himself. This statement is

> identical with the statement that the society of this estranged man is the caricature of a true community, of his true species-existence ... his activity is a torment to him, his own creation confronts him as an alien power, his wealth appears as poverty, the essential bond joining him to other men appears inessential, in fact separation from other men appears to be his true existence, his life appears as the sacrifice of his life, the realization of his essence appears as the de-realization of his life, his production is the production of nothing, his power over objects appears as the power of objects over him; in short, he, the lord of creation, appears as the servant of that creation.[19] ...
>
> In a situation based on exchange, labour immediately becomes wage-labour. ... Wage-labour and the product of the worker does not stand in any direct relation to his wants and to his vocation, but in both respects is determined by social configurations alien to the worker. ... As value, exchange value, equivalent, the product is no longer produced on account of its direct personal connection with the producer.[20] ...
>
> It thus becomes wholly accidental and unimportant whether the relationship between producer and product is governed by immediate enjoyment and personal needs and whether the *activity*, the act of working, involves the fulfilment of his personality, the realization of his natural talents and spiritual goals.[21]

Marx asserts a connection between private property, exchange, and the division of labour:

> Thus the more developed and important is the power of society within private property, the more man is *egoistic*, unsocial and estranged from his own essence.

> Just as the reciprocal exchange of the produce of human activity appears as barter, horse-trading, so the reciprocal complementing and exchange of human activity itself appears in the form of: the *division of labour*. This makes man, as far as is possible, an abstract being, a lathe, etc., and transforms him into a spiritual and physical abortion.[22]

Marx compares the horror of production for exchange in which man is worthless to man with production when money is not involved, and hence private property is not involved likewise.

> Let us suppose that we had produced as human beings. In that event each would have doubly affirmed himself and his neighbour in his production. (1) In my production I would have objectified the specific character of my individuality and for that reason I would both have enjoyed the expression of my own individual life during my activity and also, in contemplating the object, I would experience an individual pleasure . . . [23] (2) In your use or enjoyment of my product I would have the immediate satisfaction and knowledge that in my labour I had gratified a human need . . . (3) I would have acted for you as the mediator between you and the species, thus I would be acknowledged by you as the complement of your own being, as an essential part of yourself. I would thus know myself to be confirmed both in your thoughts and your love.[24]

The misery of wage-labour is therefore not essentially a matter of poverty which might be alleviated by an increase in wages:

> An enforced rise in wages . . . would therefore be nothing more than better pay for slaves and would not mean an increase in human significance or dignity for either the worker or the labour. . . .

> Wages are an immediate consequence of estranged labour, and estranged labour is the immediate cause of private property. If the one falls then the other must fall too.[25]
>
> ... the emancipation of society from private property, etc., is expressed in the political form of the emancipation of the workers. ... in their emancipation is contained universal human emancipation. The reason ... is that the whole of human servitude is involved in the relation of the worker to production, and all relations of servitude are nothing but modifications and consequences of this relation.[26]

The emancipation Marx knows as communism which

> is the positive supersession of private property as human self-estrangement, and hence the true appropriation of the human essence through and for man; it is the complete restoration of man to himself as a social, i.e. human, being. ... This communism is ... the genuine resolution of the conflict between man and nature and between man and man.[27] ...
>
> The positive supersession of *private property*, as the appropriation of human life, is therefore the positive supersession of all estrangement, and the return of man from religion, the family, the state, etc., to his human, i.e. social existence.[28]

When private property is abolished – as it has to be – division of labour is also abolished. This state of affairs is described in a famous passage in *The German Ideology*:

> in communist society, where nobody has one exclusive sphere of activity but each can become accomplished in any branch he wishes, society regulates the general production and thus makes it possible for me to do one thing today and another tomorrow, to hunt in the morning, fish in the afternoon, rear cattle in the evening,

criticise after dinner, just as I have a mind, without ever becoming hunter, fisherman, herdsman or critic.[29]

But what is politics before Communism? It is no more than a version of the Hobbesian state of nature. 'Political power properly so-called, is merely the organized power of one class for oppressing another.'[30] If the proletariat should have the upper hand over the bourgeoisie then it will have to take measures such as the following:

1. Abolition of property in land and application of all rents of land to public purposes.
2. A heavy progressive or graduated tax.
3. Abolition of all right of inheritance.
4. Confiscation of the property of all emigrants and rebels.
   etc.

Who whom. The alpha and omega of politics and political science for Marx.

I have now examined the political thought of Hegel *and* Marx, both in the sense of showing *how*, by what mediation, the thought of Hegel became the thought of Marx; and in the sense of *comparing* the thought of Hegel with the thought of Marx.

In the Eighteenth Brumaire of Louis Napoleon, Marx wrote: 'Hegel remarks somewhere that all facts and personages of great importance in world history occur, as it were, twice. He forgot to add: the first time as tragedy, the second as farce. Caussidière for Danton, Louis Blanc for Robespierre, the Montagne of 1848 to 1851 for the Montagne of 1793 to 1795, the nephew for the uncle.' You might consider whether the list should be extended, by comparing not only the uncle with the nephew, but also one particular contemporary of Napoleon I with one particular contemporary of Napoleon III.

## Notes

1. Marx, *Early Writings*, p. 397.
2. Ibid., p. 61.
3. Ibid., p. 62.
4. Ibid., pp. 62–3.
5. Ibid., p. 87.
6. Ibid., p. 85.
7. Ibid., p. 87.
8. Ibid., p. 89.
9. Marx and Engels, *The German Ideology*, part I, ed. C. J. Arthur (London, Lawrence and Wishart 1970), pp. 57–8.
10. Ibid., p. 106.
11. Ibid., p. 79.
12. Ibid., p. 80.
13. Karl Marx, *The Communist Manifesto*, included in *The Revolutions of 1848, Political Writings*, vol. I, edited and introduced by David Fernbach (London, Allen Lane, 1973), p. 69.
14. *The German Ideology*, pp. 64–5.
15. Ibid., pp. 58–9.
16. Marx, *Early Writings*, p. 260.
17. Ibid.
18. Ibid., p. 261.
19. Ibid., pp. 265–6.
20. Ibid., p. 268.
21. Ibid., p. 269.
22. Ibid.
23. Analogue of Schiller and Hölderlin.
24. Marx, *Early Writings*, p. 277.
25. Ibid., p. 333. All wages are the wages of sin.
26. Ibid., pp. 332–3.
27. Ibid., p. 348.
28. Ibid., p. 349.
29. *The German Ideology*, p. 53.
30. *Communist Manifesto*, pp. 86–7.

# AFTERWORD: HEGEL IN THE MIDDLE EAST

(1) The question which I have asked myself and which I want to explore in this talk is what Hegel would have made of Middle Eastern politics now.

(2) It is not a fanciful question to ask. From his earliest youth Hegel was passionately interested in current politics.

An enthusiast for the French Revolution. Political conditions in the Pays de Vaud. Frankfurt pamphlet on the domestic affairs of Württemburg and the much larger essay on the German Constitution, both concerned with the current political situations in the German-speaking world and in his own duchy.

Almost the last thing he wrote was a long article of 1831 on the English Reform Bill.

Newspaper editor in Bamberg for a year – and much interested, as his letters show, in what is involved in running a newspaper.

The newspaper is modern man's equivalent of morning prayer.

(3) So that there is little doubt that had he been alive today, he would have been as avidly interested in the affairs of a world which the scientific energy, the military power and the political activity of Hegel's own Europe has revolutionized and unified, as he was in the predominantly European concerns which filled the newspapers of his day.

(4) Since Hegel is not now alive, we have to adopt some stratagem in order to elicit what he might have to say about the Middle East in our own day. And the best stratagem it seems to me would consist in asking what view Hegel takes of political life in the modern state and in asking further whether the features of this modern state are present in the political structures currently existing in the Middle East. And if they are not present, how Hegel would look upon those features which he might identify as being undoubtedly present.

(5) About such a stratagem there is nothing arbitrary or artificial or fanciful. For Hegel was not only interested in current politics. He is also the author of the *Philosophy of Right*, which he published in 1821 and which was the last philosophical treatise which he himself published. It is not only the last philosophical treatise to be written by Hegel, but I think that it is the last philosophical treatise – so far – in European intellectual history to attempt to give a coherent and systematic account of the character of a modern European state and of the organizing ideas which must underlie such a state.

(6) I want now briefly to consider some of the ideas which Hegel puts before us in his treatise and which might help us to answer the question we are considering.

A good summary of Hegel's whole argument in the *Philosophy of Right* is a short paragraph which stands almost at the beginning of the work:

> The basis of right is in the general mind; its precise place and point of origin is the will. The will is free, so that freedom is both the substance of right and its goal, while the system of right is the realm of freedom made actual, the world of mind brought forth out of itself like a second nature. (para 4)

It is no exaggeration to say that the *Philosophy of Right* is an exposition, an explication, an amplification of this paragraph. This of course we cannot possibly do here, nor do we want to do it. But from this paragraph we will take up and particularly emphasize a few relevant points:

> System of right is the political system or structure.
> The basis of this, says Hegel, is mind and its 'precise place and point of origin is the will'.
> Will entails mind. To will is to have the capacity to take a decision.
> To take a decision is to engage in intelligent activity.
> Will is not an overmastering impulse or blind instinct. It goes hand in hand with intelligence, with mind.
> Will and mind characterize men, but no other beings in the world.
> If men have will and mind it must follow that freedom is their essence.
> (a) What a man decides is something that cannot be foreseen.
> (b) A man can decide something today and reverse his decision tomorrow.
> (c) The sum of his past decisions do not determine or define or circumscribe a human being – mind and will are perpetually restless, inventive, uncircumscribed and self-transcending. This is what it means to say that a man is free.

(7) But if man is in his essence a free being, it does not follow that man has always known this about himself, or that men have always known how to organize and operate institutions which make manifest and actual the freedom which is inherent and potential in them. In fact, one of the things which Hegel wishes to establish in the *Philosophy of Right* is that only in modern times in what we would call Western Europe has the possibility emerged of (to use the words of paragraph 4 which I

quoted earlier) the realm of freedom being made actual – actual in institutions, laws and modes of behaviour.

(8) The realm of freedom made actual is, then, not something which happens suddenly and all at once; again, it is not something which a man or even a number of men can plan for, no matter where they are placed in time and space. The realm of freedom made actual is the outcome of human history over many centuries and generations, the potential which can reveal itself as actual only over time. For Hegel, then, history has a meaning, and the meaning may be summed up in the title of a well-known book by the well-known Italian Hegelian, Benedetto Croce: *History as the Story of Liberty*.

(9) The stages of this history seen as the progressive manifestation of human freedom in actuality are worked out by Hegel in the *Lectures on the Philosophy of History*, which is probably the best-known, most accessible and most popular of his works, and which was edited from Hegel's manuscript and notes by his students and first published posthumously in 1837 by a disciple and friend. I may say in passing that the introduction to these lectures, entitled by the editor, Hoffmeister, *Reason in History*, much enlarged by the addition of material from Hegel's manuscript, published in 1955 (and in an English translation by the Cambridge University Press in 1975) is for the non-philosophical reader probably the best introduction to Hegel's thought on politics and history.

(10) Briefly, to use a formula of his, these stages are those in which first one, then some, and lastly all know they are free. These stages are those to be found in the Oriental, the Greek and the Roman, and what Hegel calls the Germanic realms, respectively. From the context

it is clear that by Germanic he means the populations of northwestern Europe who were the heirs of the Roman Empire in the West.

(11) These peoples come last in point of time and it is among them that now, in retrospect, we can discern institutions, habits and customs which exhibit freedom in its actuality – a society in which all men know themselves to be free and seek, of course with varying success, to actualize this freedom. In retrospect, I have said – and this is of some importance since Hegel's thought is everywhere significantly retrospective. As the conclusion of the famous preface to the *Philosophy of Right* puts it,

> It is only when actuality is mature that the ideal first appears over against the real and that the ideal apprehends this same real world in its substance and builds it up for itself into the shape of an intellectual realm. When philosophy builds its grey in grey, then, has a shape of life grown old. (Mephistopheles: 'My worthy friend, grey are all the theories / And green alone life's golden tree.') By philosophy's grey in grey, it cannot be rejuvenated but only understood. The owl of Minerva spreads its wings only with the falling of the dusk.

Hegel, then, is not a prophet or a seer, nor does he believe that philosophy which 'apprehends the . . . real world in its substance and builds it up for itself in the shape of an intellectual realm' can possibly set out to reform the world or prescribe for its ills.

(12) What, then, does Hegel see in the modern West European state which leads him to conclude that it is an actualization of freedom more than any other political arrangement which has preceded it?

Man, we have said, is in essence free – because he is mind and will. We, the philosophical observer, from our vantage point know this, but men have not always known it in its full implications. At various stages in their history men have conceived themselves to be bound by external authority, whether divine or human. It is only in modern times in Western Europe that men have come to a full realization that in the final analysis, it is a matter of their own judgement whether they choose to be bound by an external authority, and that the deliverances and ordinances of any such external authority, if they are to accept it, has to satisfy their conscience, and not to affront their moral sense. For good or ill this is the character of modern European men, and in their societies and states the consequences will perforce appear. These consequences are not always appreciable and can sometimes be terrifying. Some of the most eloquent pages of the *Philosophy of Right* are indeed devoted to the exploration of the horrors which can result from what are taken to be the promptings of conscience.

(13) There is another distinctive aspect of the modern West European which Hegel identifies. He does so in the section of his book entitled civil society – a section which is most original, and most remarkable considering that these ideas were being agitated by Hegel in his lectures when he was a *Privatdozent* at Iena in the years 1803–5. Remarkable especially for their penetration, since they dealt with a state of affairs which cannot have been very familiar in a German-speaking society which was predominantly agricultural and traditional and in which a mercantilist absolution was the order of the day. For as we quickly discover, by civil society Hegel means the market and its logic as it has become familiar to us in the economies of Western Europe. Man in civil society is the analogue of man who recognizes no morality but what his conscience enjoins. Civil society,

Hegel says (para 238), tears the individual from his family ties, estranges the members of the family from one another, and recognizes them as self-subsistent persons. Civil society, 'the achievement of the modern world' as he describes it, 'is the territory of mediation where there is free play for every idiosyncrasy, every talent, every accident of birth and fortune, and where waves of every passion gush forth, regulated only by reason glinting through them' (para 182 Add.). The reason which glints through this chaos of needs, passions, tastes, preferences, idiosyncrasies is the logic, the unpremeditated and spontaneous logic of a market which leads us to 'play into each others' hand, and so hang together' and where, therefore, 'everything private becomes something social' (para 192 Add.).

(14) These two features of modern West European man, namely the self-legislating authority of conscience and the infinity of the desires which he discovers that he can satisfy, constitute at the same time his predicament.

The predicament is this: that a collection of men who aspire to be governed by literally nothing but the dictates of their conscience will soon discover that such a mode of life must be anarchic, violent and dangerous, since the absolute dictates of one conscience will sooner rather than later come into collision with the absolute dictates of another conscience, and in the absence of a judge the conflict must go on to the point of mutual annihilation.

(15) Again, the market is not, ultimately, self-sustaining. It requires to be policed, and the quarrels of its denizens – and quarrels must arise wherever there is a buyer and a seller – must be adjudicated. But there is something much more serious: the market can produce extreme riches and extreme poverty. The extreme poverty which makes of men not the sons but the stepsons of civil society (for, as we have seen, civil society wrenches men

away from the protective cocoon of the family) creates a rabble which puts at risk the life and possessions of everyone. Riches by themselves, as we know, and as a long list of literary masterpieces from *L'Avare* to *The Great Gatsby* and beyond testify, yield in the end poor satisfaction, and may even lead to extreme spiritual impoverishment.

(16) If, then, the freedom of which man is now conscious is to be made actual, if it is not to be self-destructive or hamstrung by inherent limitations, it has to become what Hegel calls a 'system of right' – in other words a state which will give its citizens a common moral idiom and enable them to pursue their own diverse private goals and desires, while feeling secure and at home in the society of their fellow-citizens. The requirements which the modern state has to satisfy are much more difficult to meet than say those of the Greek polis or the Roman *civitas* – simply because in these political organizations the *politis* or the *civis* does not look upon himself as a centre of independent judgement, and simply has no idea of the endless and marvellous cornucopia which the dynamic modern market economy – the global supermarket – pours out for the benefit alike of duke and dustman, of Judy O'Grady and the Colonel's Lady. These requirements can only be satisfied in political societies where the bond between the citizens is not kinship or race or class or religion, but law (an impersonal and deliberate enactment), law which is itself the will of the citizens, but a will which is and has to be articulated and mediated through constitutional representative institutions, where the citizen recognizes himself and where he is at home. 'The state', in brief, 'is the world which mind has made for itself' (para 272A).

(17) Difficult and problematic as the successful functioning of such a state is, yet its principle, says Hegel, 'has prodigious strength and depth because it allows the principle of subjectivity to progress to its culmination in the extreme of self-subsistent personal particularity, and yet at the same time brings it back to the substantive unity and so maintains this unity in the principle of subjectivity itself (para 260). What is important, Hegel again says, is that 'my particular end should become identified with the universal end'. 'It has often been said', he continues in the same passage, 'that the end of the state is the happiness of the citizens. That is perfectly true. If all is not well with them, if their subjective aims are not satisfied, if they do not find that the state as such is the means to their satisfaction, then the footing of the state itself is insecure' (para 265A). The private interest and the public interest go hand in hand.

(18) I come now at last to Hegel in the Middle East. Philosophy, Hegel said, is a circle; only the circular road leads you to the truth, more – you will come to see there that the circle is the truth made manifest. As the poet Eliot puts it:

> the end of all our exploring
> Will be to arrive where we started
> And know the place for the first time.
> *(Little Gidding)*

The question, then, that we asked at the outset – namely what Hegel would have made of Middle Eastern politics now – this question answers itself.

Civil society is absent or almost absent. The primacy of the state has increased and the State is the fount of wealth. The taste and habit of submitting all decisions, all actions, all authority, all existing arrangements to the arbitrament of one's conscience – this too is something which is largely non-existent in the area, where the authority of tradition, of the ruler and very frequently of the *fait accompli* is seldom questioned. For this reason, we shall not expect to find, and will not in fact find that 'system of right' which is 'the realm of freedom made actual' – a realm in which modern man can feel both secure and at home.

All this is to say that modernity in its most essential and significant sense has hardly if at all penetrated the Middle East. This is of course not said in dispraise or disparagement of the Middle East. It is what it is and not another thing. It is what it is – but what, you might ask, is it? Something much older, much tougher, and which has certainly proved more durable and longer lasting than this comparative newcomer of the modern Western state – namely *Oriental Despotism*, K. Wittfogel: 'state stronger than society'. But there are differences between ancient and modern Oriental despotism. In a world unified by Western power and Western technology Oriental despotism has adopted the vocabulary and the aspirations associated with the Western state. But the vocabulary is not congruent with that which it aspires to describe, and the ideals must perforce remain mere ideals. This fact too is of great significance since the very attempt to realize ideals which are effectively unrealizable leads to disorder and instability which becomes cumulative. Is this then a clue to a political condition which newspapermen and their readers have learnt to describe as volatile?

# BIBLIOGRAPHY

The two translations of Hegel's work referred to throughout this series of lectures are:

*Early Theological Writings: G. W. F. Hegel*, translated by T. M. Knox and with an introduction and fragments translated by Richard Kroner, Philadelphia, University of Pennsylvania Press, 1981

*Hegel's Philosophy of Right*, trans. with notes by T. M. Knox, Oxford, Oxford University Press, 1945

Some of the other works by Hegel referred to in the text can be found in:

*Hegel's Political Writings*, trans. T. M. Knox, ed. Z. A. Pelczynski, Oxford, Oxford University Press, 1964

Other translations consulted include:

*The Phenomenology of Mind*, trans. J. B. Baillie, London, George Allen & Unwin, 1971

*G. W. F. Hegel: L'esprit du christianisme et son destin*, with an introduction by J. Hyppolite, trans. J. Martin, Paris, Librairie Vrin

Other works by Hegel mentioned in the text include the following:

*The Difference between the Philosophical Systems of Fichte and Schelling*, 1801
*Folk Religion and Christianity*, ed. Nohl
*Fragment of a System*
*Love*
*The Positivity of the Christian Religion*, ed. Nohl
*Realphilosophie I 1803–4*
*Realphilosophie II 1805–6*
*On the Scientific Ways of Dealing with Natural Law*
*System der Sittlichkeit 1803*
Hegel and Schelling *Faith and Knowledge*

Hegel and Schelling *On the Scientific Manner of Studying Natural Law*

**Other books referred to include:**

Althusser, Louis, trans. *Ludwig Feuerbach – Manifestes philosophiques*, Presses Universitaires de France, Paris, 1960

Arvon, Henri *Ludwig Feuerbach ou la transformation du sacré*, Paris, Presses Universitaires de France, 1957

Asveld, P. *La pensée religieuse du jeune Hegel*, Louvain, Publ. Univ., 1953

Avineri, Shlomo 'Labor, Alienation, and Social Classes in Hegel's *Realphilosophie*' in *The Legacy of Hegel: Proceedings of the Marquette Hegel Symposium 1970*, The Hague, Martinus Nijhoff, 1973.

Bauer, Bruno *Christianity Uncovered*, 1843

Beaumarchais *The barbier de Séville*, 1775

— *Le mariage de Figaro*, 1784 [English trans. 1785]

Brazill, William J. *The Young Hegelians*, New Haven and London, Yale University Press, 1970

Cart, Jean-Jacques *Confidential Letters Concerning the Former Constitutional Relation of the Wadtland (Pays de Vaud) to the State of Berne. A Complete Exposition of the Earlier Oligarchy of the Berne Nobility*

Chamley, Paul *Economie Politique et Philosophie chez Stewart et Hegel*, Paris, 1963

Diderot *Le Neveu de Rameau*

Dilthey, Wilhelm *Die Jugendgeschichte Hegels*, ed. H. Nohl, 2nd edn., 1959

Eliot, T. S. *Collected Poems 1909–1962*, London, Faber & Faber, 1963

Ferguson, Adam *An Essay on the History of Civil Society*, 1767 [German trans. *Versuch über die Geschichte der Bürgerlichen Gesellschaft*, 1768] edited with an introduction by Duncan Forbes, Edinburgh, Edinburgh University Press, 1978. A reprint of the first, 1767 edition, collated with the 1814 edition

Feuerbach 'Contribution to the Critique of Hegel's Philosophy' in *Halle Annals*

— *The Essence of Religion*

— *Provisional Theses for the Reform of Philosophy*

— *Of Reason, One, Universal, Infinite*

— *Thoughts on Death and Immortality*, 1830

— *Principles of the Philosophy of the Future*, 1843

— *The Essence of Christianity,* 1841
Fitzgerald, F. Scott *The Great Gatsby,* 1926
Harris, H. S. *Hegel's Development: Toward the Sunlight 1770–1801,* Oxford, Clarendon Press, 1972
Haym, Rudolf *Hegel and his Times,* 1857
Hess, Moses 'The Essence of Money' in *German-French Annals*
Hölderlin, Friedrich *His Poems,* trans. Michael Hamburger with a critical study of the poet, London, The Harvill Press, 1952
— *Hyperion,* trans. Willard R. Trask, A Signet Classic, New York and Toronto, The New American Library, 1965
d'Hondt, Jacques *Hegel secret, recherches sur les sources cachées de la pensée de Hegel,* Paris, Presses Universitaires de France, 1968
— *Hegel en son Temps (Berlin 1818–1831),* Paris, 1968
Jacobi, F. H. *Ueber die Lehre des Spinoza in Briefen an der Herrn Moses Mendelssohn* [*Letters to Moses Mendelssohn on the Teaching of Spinoza*], Breslau, 1785
Kaan, André, trans. *G. W. F. Hegel, Le Droit naturel,* Paris, Gallimard, 1972
Kamenka, Eugene *The Philosphy of Ludwig Feuerbach,* London, Routledge & Kegan Paul, 1970
Kant *Critique of Practical Reason,* trans. T. K. Abbott
— *Religion within the Bounds of Reason Alone,* 1793
Kaufmann, Walter 'The Hegel Myth and its Method' in Kaufmann (ed.), *Hegel's Political Philosophy,* New York, 1970
Kedourie, E. *Nationalism,* 3rd edn., London, Hutchinson, 1966. Fourth, expanded edition published in 1993 by Blackwell, Oxford
Lessing, G. E. *Die Erziehung des Menschengeschlechts,* Berlin, 1780 [*The Education of the Human Race,* contained in *The Laocoon and Other Prose Writings of Lessing,* trans. and ed. W. B. Rönnfeldt, London, Walter Scott Ltd., 1895]
— *Ernst und Falk*
— *Nathan der Weise,* 1779
McLellan, David *The Young Hegelians and Karl Marx,* London, Macmillan, 1969
Marx, Karl *Early Writings,* introduced by Lucio Colletti, trans. Rodney Livingstone and Gregor Benton, London, Penguin Books, 1975
— *Capital*
— *The Communist Manifesto* included in *The Revolutions of 1848, Political Writings,* vol. I. Edited and introduced by David Fernbach, London, Allen Lane, 1973

— 'A Contribution to the Critique of Hegel's Philosophy of Right. Introduction' in *Franco-German Yearbooks*, 1844
— *Critique of Hegel's Dialectic and General Philosophy*
— *Critique of Hegel's Doctrine of the State*
— *Critique of Political Economy*
— *The Economic and Philosophical Manuscripts*, 1844
— *Ludwig Feuerbach and the End of Classical German Philosophy*, 1888
— *Theses on Feuerbach*, 1845

Marx, Karl and Friedrich Engels *The German Ideology*, ed. C. J. Arthur, London, Lawrence and Wishart, 1970
— *The Communist Manifesto*

Mosheim *Institutiones historiae ecclesiasticae* (1726) [*Ecclesiastical History*], 1764

Mueller, G. E. *Hegel: The Man, His Vision and Work*, New York, Pageant Press Inc., 1968

Papaioannou, Kostas *Hegel*, Paris, Editions Seghers, 1962

Plato *The Republic*

Quesnai *Philosophie rurale*

Reimarus, Hermann Samuel *An Apology for the Rational Worshippers of God* (The Wolfenbüttel Fragments)

Rousseau, Jean-Jacques *Discours sur l'origine de l'inégalité*, 1755

Schiller, Friedrich *On the Aesthetic Education of Man: In a Series of Letters*, ed. and trans. with Introduction, Commentary and Glossary by Elizabeth M. Wilkinson and L. A. Willoughby, Oxford, Clarendon Press, 1967
— *Collected Poems*

Steuart, Sir James *An Inquiry into the Principles of Political Oeconomy: Being an Essay on the Science of Domestic Policy in Free Nations*, edited with an introduction by Andrew S. Skinner, 2 vols., Edinburgh and London, 1966

Strauss, David *Life of Jesus*, trans. Marion Evans [George Eliot, pseud.] London, John Chapman, 1854

Valéry, Paul *Poems*, trans. David Paul, London, Routledge & Kegan Paul, 1971

Wittfogel, Karl *Oriental Despotism: A Comparative Study of Total Power*, 1957

# INDEX

absolute freedom   99
absolute knowledge   74, 75
absolute objectivity   108
abstraction   176
alienation   174
  in civil society   186
  of human essence   26, 160, 172, 173
  of labour   186
  Marx on   186
  money and   160–1
Althusser, Louis   164n
analytical philosophy   6
anthropology   157
anthropotheism   159
Aquinas, St Thomas   157
Arvon, Henri   164n, 165n
Avineri, Shlomo   128n

Bakunin, Mikhail   159
Bauer, Bruno   150
  *Christianity Uncovered*   159
Beaumarchais, Pierre de   14
beauty, Schiller on   28, 33
Boccaccio, Giovanni   38
Booker, Christopher   137
Bradley, Francis Herbert   52
Brazill, William J.   164n, 165n
Brethren of the Free Spirit   67–8
Buddhism   53
Butler, E. M.   30

*Capital*   148, 161, 169–70, 171, 175, 186

Cart, Jean-Jacques   11
caste system   125, 132
Chamley, Paul   116, 122, 127
Christianity
  Christian love   86, 91, 122
  *en kai pan* and   61
  Feuerbach on   152–64
  Hegel on   12, 25, 43, 69, 79, 82–3, 86, 88, 91–103 *passim*, 148–50
  Kant and   92, 93–4
  Lessing on   51: Wolfenbüttel Fragments   40–1
  as positive religion   86, 94
  Reimarus on   40–1
  subjectivity and   96
  the Trinity   50
  *see also* God, Jesus, religion
civil society   124, 130–41, 180, 200
  alienation in   186
  class-divisions   125–6, 127, 132, 135
  colonization and   127
  corporations   138, 143–4
  dependency and   131–2
  division of labour and   126
  family and   132, 143, 144–5, 180, 181, 197, 198, 199
  institutionalized violence   134
  labour and   115–29, 136
  laws   134

civil society (*cont.*):
  as market   133, 180, 197, 198
  Marx on   183–6
  needs and   124, 131–2
  poverty in   126, 127, 135–6, 138
  proletariat, creation of   136
  property and   110
  specialization and   126
  state and   140, 184–5
  subjective desire and   133
  wants, creation of   134–5
  wealth in   136–8
civilization, Schiller on   19, 20, 23–4
class-divisions   125–6, 132, 135
  needs and   125
  poverty and   127
Coleridge, Samuel Taylor   28
Colletti, Lucio   165
colonization   127
commodity exchange   123
commodity fetishism   26, 161
communism   189–90
*Communist Manifesto, The*   169, 183
conscience   96, 98, 104, 197
consciousness   112–13, 181, 186
  Feuerbach on   155
  Hegel on   74, 143, 146
  Marx on   171–2, 176, 179, 184
  of the master   112–13
  self-consciousness   70, 98, 159, 173, 176
  of the slave   112–14
  social existence and   171, 179
constitution
  as divine   146, 147

  Marx on   183
Corneille, Thomas   114
corporations   138, 143–4
Cousin, Victor   9
*Critique of Hegel's Dialectic and General Philosophy*   166, 167
*Critique of Hegel's Doctrine of the State*   3, 169, 177
*Critique of Political Economy*   170–1, 176, 179
Croce, Benedetto   195

dance, Schiller on   28–9
democracy, Marx on   183
dependency   131–2
  *see also*   needs
d'Hondt, Jacques   7
Diderot, Denis   14
*Difference between the Philosophical systems of Fichte and Schelling*   4, 13, 96
Dilthey, Wilhelm   8, 104
Disraeli, Benjamin   41
division of labour   135, 186, 187, 188
  abolition of   189–90
  civil society and   126
  exchange and   187–8
  private property and   187–8

*Early Theological Writings*   4
*Early Writings*   165n
*Economic and Philosophical Manuscripts*   3, 163–4, 166, 167, 169, 172–3, 177, 179, 180, 186
economics   115–28
education, Lessing on   44, 46, 49
*Eleusis*   65–6
Eliot, T. S.   52, 59, 64, 200
Emerson, Ralph Waldo   52–3

*en kai pan* (one and all)  48–62, 65, 69, 73
  and Christianity  61
  Hölderlin and  56–61, 65
  Lessing and  48–55
Engels, Friedrich  150, 159–60, 183
'The English Reform Bill'  2
Epicurus  107
equality, needs and  124
essence
  human, alienation of  26, 160, 172, 173
  labour as  175
evil will  99, 100–1
exchange, production for  187–8
exchange economy  119–21
exchange-value  186
existence, Marx on  176

faith  71–2, 73
*Faith and Knowledge*  13
family
  civil society and  132, 143, 144–5, 180, 181, 197, 198, 199
  piety  139
  state and  142, 144–5
Ferguson, Adam  140n
fetishism of commodities  26, 161
Feuerbach, Ludwig  18, 26, 46, 150
  anthropology  157
  on Christianity  152–64
  on consciousness  155
  *Essence of Christianity, The*  26, 150, 154, 156, 160
  on God  26, 157–8, 172, 173
  God-man  155–6, 159
  Hegel and  152–65, 173, 181
  on man  154, 155, 176–7
  Marx and  5, 18, 160, 172, 186
  on nature  163
  *Principles of the Philosophy of the Future*  150, 156, 160, 172
  *Provisional Theses for the Reform of Philosophy*  150, 157, 160, 162–3, 172
  on reason  153
  species  155, 157
  *Thoughts on Death and Immortality*  153, 154, 159
  Young Hegelians and  158–9
Fichte, J. G.  5, 6, 18, 97, 102
'Folk-Religion and Christianity'  77
*Franco-German Yearbooks*  3
freedom
  Hegel on  100, 193, 195, 196–7
  labour and  114, 130
  property and  106–7
Freemasons  41–2
French Revolution  13–14

*Geist*  70, 74–5, 122
*German Constitution, The*  115, 139
*German Ideology, The*  183, 186, 189–90
*German-French Annals*  160, 167
Germany  15–17
  Greek influence on  15, 30
God
  as alienated essence of man  26, 160, 172, 173

God (*cont.*):
  Feuerbach on  26, 157–8, 172, 173
  Hegel on  69–73, 84–5, 146–7, 149, 173
  invented by man  26
  Jesus as son of  69–72
  Kant on  17
  Lessing and  49–51, 54: revelation  44, 46, 49
  personal  53
  Spinoza on  53, 54
  the Trinity  50
  unity of  49–51
  *see also* Christianity, Jesus, religion
God-man  155–6, 159
Goethe, J. W. von  14, 54, 55, 56
Greece
  Hegel and  10, 32–3, 79–84
  Hölderlin and  31–2, 56–61, 69
  influence on German thought  15, 30
  Plato's *Republic*  107, 109, 132
  religion in  81, 82–3, 87, 88, 89
  Schiller and  20, 21, 30–2, 33

*Halle Annals*  162
Harris, H. S.  89n
Haym, Rudolf,  *Hegel and his Times*  6
Hegel
  Christianity and  12, 25, 43, 69, 79, 82–3, 86, 88, 91–103 *passim*, 148–50
  on civil society *see* civil society
  on consciousness  74, 143, 146
  on economics  115–16
  education of  10, 12
  Feuerbach and  152–65, 173, 181
  on freedom  100, 193, 195, 196–7
  on God  69–73, 84–5, 146–7, 149, 173
  on history  195
  influences on  10–22: Adam Smith  12, 115; French Revolution  13–14; Greece  10, 32–3, 79–84; Hölderlin  10, 18; Jacobi  56; Kant  17, 18, 92, 93, 95; Lessing  18, 34, 36–47; Mosheim  67–8; Schiller  18, 23–35; Sir James Steuart  12, 115–23
  on Jesus  25, 69–74, 82, 85–9, 91–2, 94–6
  letter to Schelling  4–5, 8, 10, 12, 13, 14, 18, 28, 37, 42, 96
  on man  176
  Marx on  166–91
  on mind  143, 193, 194, 196
  on nature  174, 175, 181
  on personality *see* personality
  political oppression  92–3
  on positivity  25–6, 44, 85–6, 91, 92–3
  on property *see* property
  religion and  4, 12, 26, 67–74, 77–103: objective and subjective distinguished  77–8; positive religion  25–6, 44, 85–6, 91, 92–3
  on the state *see* state

## Index

Hegelianism 7, 64
Herder, J. G. 15
Hess, Moses 160, 186
Hinduism 53
history
   dialectical view of 43
   Hegel on 195
   Lessing on 43, 44, 46, 48
   Marx on 184–5
   philosophy of 37, 43
Hoffmeister, Johannes 195
Hölderlin, Friedrich 11, 14, 37, 42–3, 64
   *Archipelago, The* 57
   *Bread and Wine* 60–1, 69
   *en kai pan* and 56–61, 65
   Greece and 31–2, 56–61, 69
   Hegel, influence on 10, 18
   *Hyperion* 56–60, 67
   Lessing, influence of 46
human essence, alienation of 26, 160, 172, 173
humanism, Marxism as 46, 55
Hyppolite, J. 90n

Idea 139, 176, 181, 182–3, 186
Iena lectures 63, 104, 115, 123, 126–7, 130
institutionalized violence 134
irritability 143
Islam 39, 41, 53

Jacobi, F. H. 54, 56
Jesus
   Hegel on 25, 69–74, 82, 85–9, 91–2, 94–6
   Lessing on 45
   Reimarus on 40–1
   as son of God 69–72
   Strauss on 150, 155–6

Wolfenbüttel Fragments 40–1
*see also* Christianity, God, religion
Judaism 39, 41, 44, 69, 93

Kaen 103n
Kamenka, Eugene 164n, 165n
Kant
   Christianity and 92, 93–4
   *Critique of Practical Reason* 26
   Fichte and 5
   on God 17
   Hegel, influence on 17, 18, 92, 93, 95
   moral theory 26, 36, 97, 99–100, 101
   *Religion within the Bounds of Reason Alone* 92, 93
   Schiller and 26, 36
Kaufmann, Walter 7
Kedourie, E. 151
Kierkegaard, Søren 149–50
Knox, T. M. 2, 4, 90n, 102n, 103n, 141n, 146
Kroner, Richard 4, 90n, 102n, 103n

labour
   alienation of 186
   civil society and 115–29, 136
   dehumanization and 126–7
   as essence 175
   estranged 189
   freedom and 114, 130
   man's objectification in 123
   master and slave 111–14, 120, 130
   nature and 105
   needs and 123

labour (*cont.*):
  Schiller on  23
  wage-labour  187, 188–9
*Lectures on the Philosophy of History*  195
Left Hegelians  150, 154, 156, 162, 168
Lessing, G. E.
  on education  44, 46, 49
  *Education of the Human Race*  14–15, 37, 44, 46, 54, 57, 64
  *Ernst und Falk*  41, 43
  on God  49–51, 54
  *Hamburgische Dramaturgie*  40
  Hegel, influence on  18, 34, 36–47
  on history  43, 44, 46, 48
  Hölderlin, influence on  46
  on human progress  44–5
  on Jesus  45
  *Nathan the Wise*  37–9, 43, 78
  'one and all'  48–55
  pantheism  53
  Reimarus and  40–1
  on revelation  44, 46, 49
  Schelling, influence on  46
  Spinoza and  53–4, 55
  Wolfenbüttel Fragments  40–1
life  70
*Logic*  176, 179
logical positivism  6
love  122, 130
  Christian  86, 91, 122
  property and  108–9
  self-love  119
Lubac, Father de  154

McLellan, David  164n

man
  Feuerbach on  154, 155, 176–7
  Hegel on  176
  Marx on  176–7
  self-consciousness  70, 98, 159, 173, 176
  as species being  155
market
  civil society as  133, 180, 197, 198
  law and justice in  134
  poverty and  198
Marx
  on alienation  187
  on civil society  183–6
  commodity fetishism  26, 161
  communism  189–90
  on consciousness  171–2, 176, 179, 184
  on the constitution  183
  on democracy  183
  exchange-value  186
  on existence  176
  Feuerbach and  5, 18, 160, 172, 186
  on Hegel  166–91
  on history  184–5
  on man  176–7
  on nature  176
  on *Phenomenology of Mind*  166, 180
  on *Philosophy of Right*  3, 167, 179, 180–1, 183–4
  on political power  190
  production for exchange  187–8
  on property  183
  on religion  183
  on the state  183, 184
  use-value  186

Marxism
  as humanism  46, 55
  as ideology  7–8
  Promethean character
    of  55–6
master and slave  111–14, 115,
  120, 130
  consciousness and  112–14
Mendelssohn, Moses  37–8
Mill, James  186
mind
  Hegel on  143, 193, 194,
    196
  powers of  104–5
  state as mind
    objectified  140
money
  alienation and  160–1
  domination by  161
Moore, G. E.  6
moral autonomy  84, 85, 91,
  94
morality  93
  Kant on  26, 36, 97, 99–
    100, 101
  Schiller on  24–5, 27, 36
  self-determination and  99
  subjectivity and  96
Mosheim, *Ecclesiastical History*  67–8

nature
  confrontation with  105,
    123
  Feuerbach on  163
  Hegel on  174, 175, 181
  labour and  105
  Marx on  176
  personality and  105–6
  Schiller on  19, 24, 25, 27–8,
    36
Neander, J. A. W.  152

needs
  civil society and  124, 131–2
  class-divisions and  125
  community of  123
  equality and  124
  labour and  123
  system of  124–5, 132, 133
  *see also* dependency
Nohl, Hermann  4, 8, 25, 77

objectivity  99, 125, 133
  absolute  108
'On the Recent Domestic Affairs
  of Württemberg'  2, 11
*On the Scientific Manner of
  Studying Natural Law*  13
'one and all' *see en kai pan*

pantheism  53, 66–7, 147, 181
patriotism  144
Pelczynski, Z. A.  2–3, 141n
Persephone  65, 66
personality
  nature and  105–6
  Plato and  107
  and property  104–14
*Phenomenology of Mind*  6,
  13, 14, 70, 74, 96, 97, 120
  Marx on  166, 180
  master and slave  111–14,
    115, 130
philosophy of history  37, 63
*Philosophy of Right*  3, 6, 8, 9,
  63, 146, 147, 148, 175,
  193–4, 196
  civil society  124, 131, 134–
    5
  commodity exchange  123
  individual conscience  96,
    98, 197
  Marx on  3, 167, 179, 180–
    1, 183–4

*Philosophy of Right (cont.):*
  needs   123
  property   107
  vaporization   97
  wants, creation of   134–5
  will   100, 193–4
Plato
  personality and   107
  private property and   107
  *Republic*   107, 109, 125, 132
plebs *see* proletariat
*Political Writings*   2
Popper, Karl   7
positivity
  in religion   25–6, 44, 85–6, 91, 92–3: Christianity 86, 94
  Schiller on   25–6
*Positivity of the Christian Religion, The*   25, 82, 91, 92, 93, 94
possession   106, 109
  property distinguished   110–11
poverty   102, 135–6
  civil society and   126, 127
  class and   127
  market and   198
private property
  abolition of   189
  division of labour and   187–8
  exchange and   187–8
  Marx on   186, 187, 188, 189
  Plato and   107
production for exchange   187–8
proletariat   190
  creation of   136
property
  civil society and   110

  freedom and   106–7
  love and   108–9
  Marx on   183
  personality and   104–14
  possession   106, 109: distinguished   110–11
  private *see* private property
  recognizability   110–11
  rights   133–4
  subjectivity and   106–7
public spirit   121–2

*Realphilosophie*   104, 123
*Realphilosophie I*   13
*Realphilosophie II*   13
reason
  Feuerbach on   153
  Schiller on   27
*Reason in History*   195
recognizability of property   110–11
Reimarus, Hermann Samuel   40–1
religion
  Christianity *see* Christianity
  faith   71–2, 73
  God *see* God
  in Greece   81, 82–3, 87, 88, 89
  Hegel and   4, 12, 26, 67–9, 77–103
  Jesus *see* Jesus
  Marx on   183
  objective and subjective distinguished   77–8
  pantheism   53, 66–7, 147, 181
  private   78
  public   78–9
  revelation   44, 46, 49
  sacrifices   107–8
  state and   139–40
*Religious Teaching of Jesus*   69

## Index

revelation 44, 46, 49
Right Hegelians 150
Rosenkrantz, Karl 115
Rousseau, Jean-Jacques 14, 144
Ruge, Arnold 186
Russell, Bertrand 6

St Just, L. A. L. F. de 144
Schelling, F. W. J. 5, 8, 10, 12, 13, 14, 18, 28, 37, 42, 96
  influence of Lessing on 46
Schiller, J. C. F. von 18, 23–35, 44, 64, 75
  on beauty 28, 33
  on civilization 19, 20, 23–4
  on dance 28–9
  *Dance, The* 28–9
  *Gods of Greece, The* 31
  Greece and 20, 21, 30–2, 33
  Hegel, influence on 18, 23–35
  Kant and 26, 36
  on labour 23
  on morality 24–5, 27, 36
  on nature 19, 24, 25, 27–8, 36
  *On the Aesthetic Education of Man* 18–22, 23, 27, 29, 36, 57
  philosophy of history 37
  on reason 27
  *The Dance* 28–9
  *The Gods of Greece* 31
  on wholeness 22, 23, 29–30
Schleiermacher, F. E. D. 152
self-consciousness 70, 98, 159, 173, 176
self-determinism 97, 99
self-knowledge 75
self-love 119
Shklar, Judith 33
slave *see* master and slave

slavery 119–20
Smith, Adam 12, 115
social class *see* class-divisions
social existence, consciousness and 159, 176
specialization 123, 126
species, Feuerbach on 155, 157
Spinoza
  on God 53, 54
  Lessing and 53–4, 55
*Spirit of Christianity and its Fate, The* 69, 85, 86, 94–5, 96, 101, 107, 115
state 138–9, 142–51, 182, 199
  civil society and 140, 184–5
  constitution 146, 147
  divinity of 147
  family and 142, 144–5
  Marx on 183, 184
  as mind objectified 140
  patriotism 144
  religion and 139–40
  as secular deity 146
  as totality of citizens 142–4
Steuart, Sir James 12
  *Inquiry into the Principles of Political Oeconomy* 115–23
Storr, G. C. 92
Strauss, David, *Life of Jesus* 150, 155–6
subjectivity 94, 99, 101, 125, 133
  Christianity and 96
  morality and 96
  property and 106–7
  of the will 96–8, 100–2
*System der Sittlichkeit* 13

Thucydides 30
Time 79, 80
Trinity, the 50

use-value   186

Valéry, Paul   51–2, 105
vaporization   97–8
*Volkgeist*   80

wage-labour   187, 188–9
  *see also* labour
Wagner, Richard   159
wants, creation of   134–5
wealth, in civil society   136–8
welfare   146–7

wholeness, Schiller on   22, 23, 29–30
Wilkinson, Elizabeth M.   22n
will   143, 193, 194, 196
  evil   99, 100–1
  indeterminacy   98–9
  subjectivity of   96–8, 100–2
  vaporization   97–8
Willoughby, L. A.   22n
Wittfogel, K.   7, 201
Wolfenbüttel Fragments   40–1

Young Hegelians   26, 158–9

use-value 186

Valéry, Paul 51–2, 105
vaporization 97–8
Volksgeist 80

wage-labour 187, 188–9
  see also labour
Wagner, Richard 159
wants, creation of 134–5
wealth, in civil society 136–8
welfare 146–7

wholeness, Schiller on 22, 23, 29–30
Wilkinson, Elizabeth M. 22n
will 143, 193, 194, 196
  evil 99, 100–1
  indeterminacy 98–9
  subjectivity of 96–8, 100–2
  vaporization 97–8
Willoughby, L. A. 22n
Wittgenstein, K. 7, 201
Wolfenbüttel Fragments 40–1

Young Hegelians 26, 158–9